BEAUTY, LOVE AND WISDOM IN PERSIAN POETRY

BEAUTY, LOVE AND WISDOM IN PERSIAN POETRY: FOUR ESSAYS

from Aṭṭār to Rūmī, Shabistarī and Ḥāfiẓ

Hossein M. Elahi Ghomshei

TRANSLATED BY
Leonard Lewisohn

Archetype

Hossein Mohyeddin Ghomshei, better known as Elahi Ghomshei, is an Iranian scholar, philosopher, author, and lecturer on literature, art, and mysticism. Born in Tehran in 1940, he graduated from the Faculty of Theology and Islamic Studies at Tehran University. He then taught Philosophy, Theology and Islamic mysticism, as well as Persian literature in various universities for many years and was at one time Director of the National Library of Iran. He has written, translated and contributed to many books, advised on cultural and art events in various institutions in Iran and abroad, and many of the numerous lectures he has delivered have reached a wide audience on Iranian television and beyond. He is himself a lover of world literature and art and the underlying universal truths and beauty they communicate.

This collection first published in 2025 by Archetype
Chetwynd House, Bartlow
Cambridge CB21 4PP

Material is included here by kind permission of the Temenos Academy, 1994, London; World Wisdom, 2015; The Institute of Ismaili Studies and IB Tauris, 2006, and IB Tauris, 2010, respectively.

ISBN 978 1 901383 56 9 PB
ISBN 978 1 901383 55 3 HB

Image credits:
Cover: Frontispiece from *Kalila wa Dimna* of Abu'l-Ma'ali Nasr Allah, Baghdad, c. 1465, Tehran, Golestan Palace Library, no. 827
p.15: *Moraqqa-e Golistan*; p.43: Golestan Palace Library
p. 81: Metropolitan Museum Fletcher Fund, 1963
p. 123: Harvard Art Museums/Arthur M. Sackler Museum, The Stuart Cary Welch Collection, Gift of Mr. and Mrs. Stuart Cary Welch in honor of the students of Harvard University and Radcliffe College, jointly owned by the Harvard Art Museums and the Metropolitan Museum of Art

Typeset by Susana Marín

CONTENTS

Preface 11

Acknowledgments 13

1. Poetics and Aesthetics in the Persian Sufi Literary Tradition 17

2. The Symphony of Rūmī: Études in Rūmī's Poetry 45

3. Of Scent and Sweetness: 'Aṭṭar and his Legacy in Rūmī, Shabistari and Ḥāfiẓ 83

4. The Principles of the Religion of Love in Classical Persian Poetry 125

Preface

The four discourses collected in the present volume give a bird's-eye view of the vast horizons of Persian literature. They go to the heart and soul of a rich and ancient literary tradition which is devoted to the expression of our most cherished human ideals: beauty, truth, and the good—the highest forms of wisdom. Devotion to such sublime values is the hallmark of all great and noble literature in the world and the divinely inspired intellectual love of such lofty ideals is the common source of all true poetry throughout the ages.

One of the most pleasing aspects of reading world literature is that if the pilgrim-reader or his translator is well acquainted with the language concerned, he will find himself everywhere at home and after a short sojourn in the visited realm, will become absorbed in the masterpieces of this newly discovered literature.

The four discourses offered here pave the way for such pilgrims to enter the field of Persian literature. The author has undertaken to present delightful images of the familiar pastures and meadows of Persian poetry before leading the reader to its delectable heights from where the pilgrim has an unobstructed view of the Elysian Fields of its poetry.

The first discourse entitled 'Poetics and Aesthetics in the Persian Sufi Literary Tradition' demonstrates the underlying structure of Persian literature which is shown to be in harmony with the constituents of human nature. The reader is introduced to such key ideas as 'the One and the Many' to open the secret doors to understanding the main messages of Persian literature and to be initiated into otherwise inaccessible Persian lyric mystifications.

The second essay centres on Rūmī and his magic flute, which like the legendary Shahrzad of *The Arabian Nights*, imparts tale after tale to enlighten the listener and lead him through the secret sanctuaries of his own soul. 'The Symphony of Rūmī' embraces a wide range of sublime mystical ideas hidden under the veils of seemingly heretical or even erotic expressions.

The third essay entitled 'Of Scent and Sweetness: 'Aṭṭār and his Legacy in Rūmī, Shabistarī and Ḥafīẓ', leads the reader through the seven wonderful cities of love so that he may taste the immortal sweets and perfume of this great mystic poet of Persia.

Finally, in the fourth essay entitled 'The Principles of the Religion of Love in Classical Persian Poetry', the reader will enter the paradisal garden of Ḥafīẓ under whose green trees run the four promised rivers of paradise: the water of life, the wine of selflessness, the honey of pure joy, and the nectar of immortality.

The author cherishes the earnest hope that the gateways to such intellectual gardens, with their nourishing and reviving streams, will thus be opened wider to the cosmopolitan explorers of these universal treasures. As Victor Hugo in his book *William Shakespeare* has so authoritatively expressed:

> *Literature nourishes civilization, poetry nourishes the ideal. That is why literature is one of the necessities of societies; and poetry is a hunger in the soul. That is why poets are the first instructors of the people and why Shakespeare must be translated in France and Molière in England. Comments must be made on them and a vast public literary domain must be created so that all the poets, philosophers, thinkers, and creators of nobility of soul can be translated, commented on, published, printed, reprinted, copied, distributed, hawked about, explained, recited, spread abroad, given to all, given cheaply, given at cost price, and given for nothing.*

Hossein M. Elahi Ghomshei
Tehran, 2022

Acknowledgments

I am deeply indebted to the late Leonard Lewisohn, a great contemporary scholar on the Persianate literary tradition as well as a still greater sincere friend and colleague, for his wonderful translation of these four discourses and for adding further notes and references where necessary. Furthermore, I am indebted to Jane Lewisohn, another earnest devotee of Persian culture and creator of the monumental 'Golha' project, as well as to Abbas Sadegh, my cordial and earnest friend, for their persistence and productive encouragement.

In the presence of an ascetic, unknown artist, early 17th century

Poetics and Aesthetics in the Persian Sufi Literary Tradition

I. Metaphysics and Aesthetics in Sufism: Beauty's Theophany in the World of Multiplicity

A Victorian traveller once remarked that Persia is a country where people walk on silk carpets and speak the language of poetry. In the same romantic vein, Iran has been called 'the land of the rose and the nightingale', those symbols, of course, of the archetypes of the 'beloved and lover', or 'beauty and love'—or, one might say, of 'aesthetics and poetics'—if we interpret the symbol of the rose in Persian literature as referring to aesthetics and the nightingale to poetics.

As if following the passion of the nightingale for the rose, the Persian Sufi poets professed themselves to be lovers of beauty, and all their poems to be but songs and hymns in praise of that transcendent Beloved. As Ḥāfiẓ put it:

> Not I alone it is who serenades the beauties
> Of rose-cheeked ladies. All around
> There are a thousand nightingales
> Who intone the same hymn.[1]

The opening lines of another ghazal by Ḥāfiẓ convey the Persian poet's eternal message—the perpetual call of beauty to rapture, communicating the nightingale's constant romance with the rose, as well as the mystical poet's ongoing aesthetic project to view all temporal beauty as a ray of the divine Splendour:

Red roses have blossomed;
Nightingales are all drunk.
Everywhere, the hue and cry of ecstasy:
    Of Sufi,
    Devotee
    Of the Eternal Now![2]

Now, rather than entering into elaborate and complicated scholarly theories about aesthetics and poetics, I will take Ḥāfiẓ's lead and play the Saki, a cupbearer who purveys a goblet of that wine of beauty which so intoxicated the nightingales of Persia that they never regained sobriety. It is that same wine to which Shabistarī's verse refers, inciting the lover of this beauty to—

Drink down that wine whose cup is the Beloved's countenance;
Imbibe a brew whose beaker is her wine-flushed, drunken eyes.[3]

Persian Sufi poetry is animated by a vision of divine beauty—that beauty which is, in the words of Keats, 'a joy forever'. This beauty is also, in the theological vocabulary of the Koran, the 'Light of the Heavens and the Earth,' the truth underlying appearance, the absolute Being, the One who is 'like unto none'.

All round the world my heart has gone
But like unto Him found no one:
There is none like Him, none like Him, none!

The perennial tale of this beauty—which is one with truth and goodness—is also reflected in the art of Persian storytelling whose stories are traditionally prefaced with this opening line drawn from the archetypal Islamic 'creation myth': 'There was one and there was no one, except God there was none (*yakī būd, yakī nabūd; ghayr az khudā hīch kas nabūd*).' Although this statement bears a superficial resemblance to similar phrases in other literature (such as our 'Once upon a time' in English, or '*Il était une fois*' in French, for instance), the Persian expression conveys a profound philosophical message as well. All Persian stories are prefaced with this phrase simply because it was recognized that *all stories occur after this story*. From a philosophical point of view, the phrase emphasizes the basic metaphysical premise that 'the Being of the One precedes the being of the many', that the existence of 'Unity' precedes the existence of 'multiplicity'. This premise is well expressed in Maghribī's verses:

> Ah, as if your face brim-filled with sun
> Is laid to plain view
> Within both worlds every atom manifests.
>
> From the shadow downcast
> By the sun of your face
> Arose all existent things.
>
> Your visage, a sun itself, cast a shadow;
> From that penumbra all phenomena appeared.
>
> Every atom is existent through a sun;
> From every atom a sun is subsistent.[4]

Just as in Islamic metaphysical thought, one speaks of the 'One' being who precedes all other beings, in Persian Sufi aesthetics one also refers to that eternal Beauty which precedes all temporal beauty. The analogical relationship between metaphysical thinking and aesthetic thought in Persian Sufism is evoked by Jāmī in the prologue to his mystic-romantic poem 'Yūsuf and Zulaykhā':

> That heart-ravishing beautiful bride was in the bridal chamber: a lovely mistress in her blissful solitude, playing the game of love with none but herself, and drinking alone the wine of her own beauty. None knew aught of her. Even the mirror had not yet reflected her countenance. But beauty cannot stand being concealed for long. Comeliness cannot bear concealment: if you close the door, she will show her face through the window.

So she pitched her tent outside the sacred precincts, showing herself within the soul and throughout creation. In every mirror her theophanic features appeared; so that everywhere her tale was told. From that effulgence a flash struck the rose and the rose cast passion into the nightingale's heart.[5]

The Persian Sufi poets did not have mere romantic entertainment in mind in the usage of erotic imagery in passages such as these. Rather, they wished to make a metaphysical point about creation, to allude to that primordial Beauty who had unveiled herself on the 'roof of contingency' (*bām-i imkān*), so that as a result of her theophany, thousands of worlds came into being. A beam of this eternal Beauty struck the rose, and the rose reflected that beauty to the nightingale, filling the distraught bird with melody, frenzy and ecstasy. This myth of aesthetic genesis—if one may so call it—is expressed by Ḥāfiẓ in a renowned verse:

By grace of the rose
The nightingale learnt the art of song;
Else, within its slender bill,
There could never be sung
Such lovely rhymes and tunes.[6]

In another verse—one of the most sublime expressions of the myth of genesis in all of Persian literature—Ḥāfiẓ provides a more explicitly metaphysical formulation of this doctrine:

In pre-eternity, a ray of your Beauty
Was shown through its theophany.
Love appeared and set the world afire.[7]

Both of the above verses have one basic message: to show how beauty gave birth to love and how love generated existence. As Jāmī in the passage cited above pointed out, this is also the eternal tale of artistic creation. The artist first witnesses beauty. This vision arouses love and, consequently, a longing to express the beauty witnessed—through love—in artistic creation. The Greek myth of the creation of Venus's son Cupid chronicles this same eroto-metaphysical and aesthetic event, and Shakespeare's words (in *Romeo and Juliet*), 'It's Cupid who rules us all', should be taken in the same context. The metaphysical allusions of this aesthetico-metaphysical creation myth of beauty, who then created the 'world of romance' through her splendour, are many and deserve our consideration.

We have seen how beauty—symbolized by Zulaykha as *Deus absconditus*—had deserted her solitude and pitched her tent in the realm of appearance. How should this be understood? Four or five different interpretations exist in Persian Sufi writings concerning the meaning of the genesis of the realm of appearance, which may be summarized as follows:

i) According to the first interpretation, 'the realm of appearance' is seen as alluding to the world of multiplicity and temporal phenomena, symbolized in Sufi poetry by the 'tresses of the Beloved', which despite their number guide the seeker to the one Beloved—to whom each and every strand of hair alludes.

ii) According to the second interpretation, appearance itself is the 'Face of God'. This interpretation is borne out by the well-known verse in the Koran which declares that, 'Wheresoever you turn your face, there is the Face of God.'

iii) The third interpretation regards appearance as a reflection of God in the mirror of non-existence. This view is illustrated by the following verse from Shabistarī's *Garden of Mystery*:

> Non-existence is a mirror, the world its reflection;
> And man is as the reflected eye of the unseen Person.[8]

iv) A fourth interpretation follows the Platonic conception which considers the realm of appearance to be but a shadow cast by the radiance of the divine Being.

v) A fifth and final interpretation regards appearance neither as veil nor shadow, but rather, as God Himself. In the words of Rūmī:

He is the rose, the meadow, the garden and spring.
There is none other than Him in all the world's garden.

So, where Shakespeare says: 'O mistress mine, where are you roaming?', the Sufis would reply that this 'mistress' is, in fact, the pre-eternal Beloved, forever roaming alone, for beside Her there is no one else in the garden of existence. This same philosophy of beauty in which the mortal exemplar appears as the celestial original one is featured in the following lines from Shakespeare's immortal sonnet:

What is your substance, whereof are you made,
That millions of strange shadows on you tend?
Since every one hath, every one, one shade,
And you, but one, can every shadow lend:
Describe Adonis and the counterfeit
Is poorly imitated after you;
On Helen's cheek all art of beauty set,
And you in Grecian times are painted new:
Speak of the spring and foison of the year,
The one doth shadow of your beauty show,
The other as your bounty doth appear;
And you in every blessed shape we know:
In all external grace you have some part
But you like none, none you, for constant heart.[9]

Perhaps the best way to illustrate the diversity yet continuity between all these various interpretations of the eternal traffic between the two realms of Unity and multiplicity, or Beauty and appearance is by means of a diagram:

According to the Sufis, the cycle of creation is divided into two halves of a circle. The upper half represents the spiritual realm. In the upper semi-circle one finds a series of ideas pointing to Transcendence and the Divine: The One, Heaven, Paradise, Light, Eternity (that

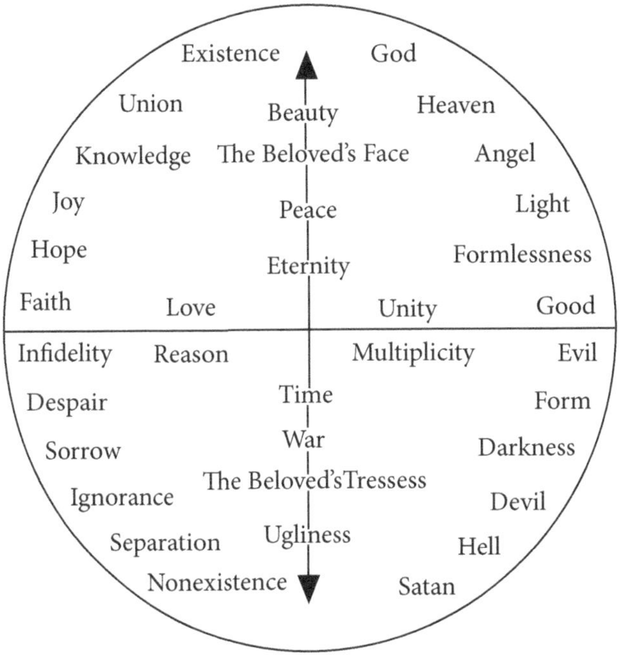

is, transcendence of time), Beauty, Peace and the Beloved's Countenance. The lower half of the circle represents the realm of multiplicity or manyness (*'ālam-i kithrat*). This, in turn, is indicated by a variety of symbols, images and concepts which reveal its inferior nature: Hell, Separation, Time, War, Satan, Heresy, Infidelity, Sorrow, and the Beloved's Tresses.

However, before exploring other dimensions of the Sufi aesthetico-poetic vision, it will be helpful to summarize the salient points of our discussion above.

First, we have seen that the central theme of Persian Sufi poetry is, in fact, the relationship between the rose and the nightingale, two poetic symbols which encode truths pertaining to all art in general. The symbol of the rose conveys allusions to concepts such as beauty, love, divine unity, poetry, music and belovedness, while the nightingale symbolizes multiplicity and diversity.

Artistic creation contains in miniature form the entire story of creation. The rose plays the part of absolute existence in this story and the nightingale—with its songs, infinitely diverse in their tonality and pitch, hymning the praise of the beauty of this divine Existence-cum-rose—expresses possible being. Incessantly, beauty—the beloved—brings into existence myriads of lovers (nightingales); every moment she contemplates herself through the eyes of these lovers, hearing them sing her praises. Instant by instant, the one beauty assumes shape after shape, harkening to a perpetual chant of panegyric intoned upon a thousand tongues. It is this Beloved, this unique One Being, and this multiplicity, to which Jāmī's lines refer:

Through all beautiful faces
You have revealed your beauty;
So, in the lover's eye
You may contemplate yourself.

Though a beloved,
You're decked out in a lover's garb;
And then your own display unto yourself
You elicit from yourself!

In this context, the above diagram of Unity and multiplicity—with the various characteristics of each half of the circle—not only furnishes us with a basis for a general theory of aesthetics and poetics in Islamic mysticism, but also expresses the basic principles of Islamic theosophy, theology and ethics. Thus, we see, for instance, how 'Satan' who belongs to the nature of 'multiplicity', and 'multiplicity' itself, are the substance of all 'war' and 'hell'. In the same way, 'Hell' is the locus of sorrow, ignorance and separation: those qualities which pertain to multiplicity. Thus, every so-called 'evil' in the end may also be subsumed under the category of 'multiplicity'. 'Ugliness', for instance, is also 'multiplicity' and 'infidelity', just as 'despair' and 'injustice' are also attributes of 'multiplicity'.

On the other—the upper—hand, 'Unity' (that is to say, 'God'), encompasses and absorbs the qualities of the lower circle by its own comprehensive qualities. Unity's most salient attribute and manifestation is found in 'love'. Love is described by the Sufis as the remedy of all ills and the alchemy of existence. Love transforms poverty to riches, pauper into prince, war into peace, ignorance into knowledge and hell into heaven.

Finally, it should be pointed out that poetry, the inspiration for which hails from the higher world of love and unity, functions as a motive and cause of unity. The therapeutic value of poetry—as well as its metaphysical motivation and aesthetic significance in Sufism—arises from this spiritual quality.

II. The Wine of Love: Aesthetic Foundations of Sufi Metaphysics

1. *The Monothematic Unity of Persian Sufi Poetry*

Between the upper and lower halves of our circle there is a constant traffic of ascent and descent: from the one to the many, and from the many back to the one. This circle of 8 not only represents the whole story of creation and the metaphysical myth of existence according to the Sufis, but also illustrates the aesthetic principle of all artistic creation. How? The Sufi, like the true creative artist, musician or poet, harbours in his heart but one single idea. When this idea 'descends', it is expressed in a multitude of words, colours, ideas, notes, symbols and images, crystallized into a form or forms which convey the sense of Unity.

According to the Sufis, the skill of the artist lies in the creative manipulation of multiplicity in order to direct the viewer's or reader's attention back to divine Unity, its transcendent source. If the artist is unsuccessful in creating a 'multiplicity' organized around Unity, the viewer/reader simply will not understand the message of his art. His work is consequently viewed as 'ugly'. Interpreted metaphysically, one could say that by disregarding the organized symmetry of divine Beauty, the artist's work is irrelevant to everything but phenomenal multiplicity. Such 'not understanding' or 'ugliness' in Sufi aesthetic theory proves that the artist's 'multiplicity' lacks any genuine foundation in Unity. Hence, any understanding of aesthetics in Sufism necessitates a complementary metaphysical understanding of divine Unity.

This infusion of Unity into multiplicity is the story of all creation, art, philosophy, religion and even science according to the Sufis. In Sufi thought, all branches of human endeavour are united in their aim to convert the many back into the one. The science of mathematics, for instance, as understood by the Sufis, acts as a comb to brush the dishevelled hair of the world of multiplicity, shaping it into Unity and revealing the underlying order in phenomena. Order implies rule and balance, qualities which reveal the one nature governing all dispersed plurality.

In their pursuit of *belles lettres*, the Sufi poets have emphasized the unity of their *intent* and the oneness of their subject-matter. Although Rūmī's work encompasses over 60,000 couplets, he still states in his *Mathnawī*:

> Our *Mathnawī* is a shop which sells only the wares of divine Unity.
> Everything else you see therein is but an idol.[10]

> This *Mathnawī* is naught but Unity within Unity.
> Soar from the earth to Arcturus, O spiritual friend.[11]

Contrary to the theories of many modern literary critics evidently unfamiliar with the unitarian aesthetic doctrine outlined above, there is only *one* theme in Persian literature. Yet, despite its monothematic nature, Sufi poetry is never monotonous or boring. In fact, one indication of the divine nature of this poetry is the fact that it always remains charming, fresh and original despite the sameness of its subject-matter. The dynamism of the monothematic subject of Persian poetry is conveyed by Sa'dī in a verse:

> Behold this wonder: Love is but one point;
> Yet every time it is mentioned, it appears new to me.[12]

Actually, this theme is not the eternal subject of Persian Sufi literature alone, but, it is, in fact, the underlying theme of all great literature. Shakespeare, in response to the accusation that his theme of love is boring and repetitious:

Why is my verse so barren of new pride,
So far from variation or quick change?
Why with the time do I not glance aside
To new-found method and to compounds strange?

gives this rejoinder:

O know, sweet-love, I always write of you
And you and love are still my argument;
So all my best is dressing old words new,
Spending again what is already spent:
    For as the sun is daily new and old,
    So is my love still telling what is told.[13]

2. The Role of Wine and Madness in Poetic Inspiration

The Sufi conception of aesthetics is inextricably linked to the concept of intoxication and wine. A proper understanding of order and unity cannot be obtained by sober means, according to the Sufis, since the external senses, being devoid of the intoxication of Love, are unable to apprehend the unified synthesis of the world of appearance with eternity.[14] Hence, the entire subject-matter of Persian poetics and aesthetics revolves around the idea of 'the wine of beauty'. However, this wine is poured into the eye, rather than the *mouth*, as Shabistarī reveals in the verse cited above:

Drink down that wine whose cup is the Beloved's countenence;
Imbibe a brew whose beaker is her wine-flushed, drunken eyes.[15]

In similar imagery Sa'dī conveys the same sentiment:

O Saki, when my turn comes for the cup,
Offer the wine to those still sober.
Leave me alone to contemplate
Dumbfounded the Saki's beauty.[16]

It is said that once Winston Churchill, having drunk heavily at a formal dinner party, was approached by a certain very respectable lady who reproached him, 'Sir, you are drunk! Very drunk! Extremely drunk! Disgustingly drunk!' Mr. Churchill calmly removed his cigar and said, 'Madame, you are ugly; very ugly; extremely ugly; disgustingly ugly! But I will be sober tomorrow.' However, the wine of the Sufi poets bears little resemblance to that enjoyed by our celebrated British statesman, from which we recover our sobriety 'tomorrow'! On the contrary, this wine so inebriates whoever imbibes it that he or she remains intoxicated until the very dawning of the Day of Judgment! Again, as Saʿdī expresses it:

> At the Call to Prayer on the eve of the Resurrection
> Only those will wake up sober who have drunk the wine
> Given at the dawn of the day of the Pre-eternal Covenant.[17]

Or, in the words of Ḥāfiẓ:

> Like me, whoever has drunk one draught
> In pre-eternity from the cup of the friend,
> Will never lift his head from drunken stupor
> Until the dawn of the Day of Judgement.[18]

Thus, the main role of intoxication is to set the drinker free from the bonds of his selfhood—the 'ego' which is the source of all multiplicity, enmity and war—and ultimately, to lead him to the realm of Unity and peace with all. Another important doctrine advocated by the Sufi poets is the 'divine lunacy' of love.

Not only is the Sufi poet a lover intoxicated with the wine of beauty, he is also a 'madman' outside the confines of convention and reason. In the mediæval Western mystical tradition, the relationship between poetry and lunacy is well expressed in Shakespeare's famous verses from *A Midsummer Night's Dream* (V.I.):

> The lunatic, the lover, and the poet
> Are of imagination all compact.

One sees more devils than vast hell can hold.
That is the madman. The lover, all as frantic,
Sees Helen's beauty in a brow of Egypt.
The poet's eye, in a fine frenzy rolling,
Doth glance from heaven to earth, from earth to heaven.
And as imagination bodies forth
The forms of things unknown, the poet's pen
Turns them to shapes, and gives to airy nothing
A local habitation and a name.
Such tricks hath strong imagination
That if it would but apprehend some joy,
It comprehends some bringer of that joy.

Considered in the light of Sufi aesthetic theory, Shakespeare's verses may be seen to allude to the mystic-lover who, when seized by the holy power of imagination, perceives in Zulaykhā a ray of the divine Beauty, just as Shakespeare's lover saw 'Helen's beauty in a brow of Egypt'. Shakespeare also alludes to the mystical poet who apprehends the name of the One within the 'airy nothing' of the many.

As regards that 'lunacy' which participates in the divine faculty of imagination, the Sufis' views seem remarkably close to those of Shakespeare as well. While the Sufi masters prided themselves on being 'lunatic', this was understood in two distinct senses: one, a lunacy *below* reason, and another, a lunacy *above* reason. The second type of lunacy, in the words of Shakespeare, is a 'fine frenzy,' whereas the first type is the neurotic or psychotic insanity belonging to the field of abnormal psychology. Thus, where Rūmī exclaims:

I am a lover, skilled in the arts of madness;
I am surfeited with culture and learning.[19]

it should be stressed that his negation of reason and his affirmation of the virtues of lunacy are *above* reason, rather than below it. This division of degrees in lunacy is also a common tenet of traditional Islamic psychology. In his *Canon of Medicine* Avicenna remarks that 'love is a sort of neurotic malady' (*al-'ishq junūn maraḍun waswasīyan*), referring to the first type of 'lunacy' which produces the external marks and effects of 'love'. However, this type of love is neurotic because it is completely self-involved. Since it is totally directed towards the gratification of egocentric desires, the emotion it arouses resembles illness, an illness which is in fact, the worst of all maladies: egotism. This is contrasted to the 'fine frenzy' of divine love, whose generous spirit gives away all it possesses to the Beloved, saving nothing for itself.[20]

3. Personifications of Inspiration in Poetry: From the Muse to the Saki

Western literary convention dictates that the poet appeal to the Muse or the Muses for inspiration. Shakespeare, thus, in one place in *Henry V* invokes: 'O, for a Muse of fire/ that would ascend the brightest heaven of invention!' In a similar manner, the Persian Sufi poet is often known as a mirror of the divine and a communer with the Muse who speaks of the mystery which is yonder. The poet is the 'tongue of the invisible realm' (*lisān al-ghayb*). Although this particular title has been officially given only to Ḥāfiẓ by posterity, it is fair to state that all other Sufi poets may equally claim it for their own. As Niẓāmī in this context opines:

> So perfect am I in the magic art of poetry
> That I am called the 'Mirror of the Invisible'.[21]

In line with the predominant monotheism of Islam, one rarely finds Sufis invoking any other muse beside God as the agent of inspiration (certainly not any of the nine Greek goddesses who presided over the arts and sciences!). Nonetheless, their message of the 'lunatic' and 'self-bereft' nature of inspiration follows a Platonic model.

In actual fact, there are two symbols in Persian Sufi poetry which correspond quite closely to the idea of the Grecian Muses. These are the Saki or *Sāqī* (the cupbearer) and the *Muṭrib* (minstrel). Just as Milton invoked his muse in the exordium of *Paradise Lost*, Ḥāfiẓ inserted into the initial verses of his 'Epistle to the Cupbearer' or *Sāqī-nāma* a plea for heavenly succour in the form of divine wine, invoking the minstrel's assistance to raise his sights to the loftier regions of the spirit. This ambivalent association between the minstrel as 'harbinger of joy' (the literal meaning of *muṭrib* in Arabic) and the divine Being appears throughout Ḥāfiẓ's *Dīwān*. Reminiscent of the opening line of Shakespeare's *Twelfth Night*, 'If music be the food of love, play on!', Ḥāfiẓ thus writes:

> How strange is the music played by love's musician!
> Every note and tune he strikes conveys us to another place![22]

Instead of minstrel and *sāqī*, God Himself is often invoked by the Persian poets as their Muse. In the prologue to *Yūsuf and Zulaykhā*, Jāmī, for instance, invokes:

> O Lord! show me but one rose of that Eternal Garden!
> Make the buds of hope bloom!
> You've made my heart a treasury of wisdom;
> You've made my tongue a scale
> To weigh precious metal and jewels.[23]

In the same sense Rūmī invokes God as his Muse to inspire his verse in these lines:

> Teach us subtle words and expressions
> Which will evoke your clemency,
> O lovely companion.[24]

Just as most Sufi poets professed to be possessed by the transcendental madness of Love, they also stressed the essentially 'selfless' nature of their poetry, claiming—albeit indirectly—the 'God-like' nature of their inspiration. In this attitude, they directly followed the doctrine of the Koran (LIII: 2-4), where, describing His Prophet, God declares:

> By the star when it plunges,
> Your comrade is not astray, neither errs,
> Nor speaks he out of caprice.
> This is naught but a revelation revealed.[25]

In fact, this same Koranic passage was often interpreted in Persian verse to allude to the idea of 'poetic selflessness', as Rūmī has commented:

> Although the Koran comes from the Prophet's lip
> Whoever says God is not its orator is an infidel.[26]

> All of these spiritual voices are from the King
> Although they issue from the throat of the Prophet.[27]

Although a difference does indeed exist between divine Revelation (*wahy*) and poetic inspiration (*ilhām*), this distinction is one of hierarchical degree, not of essential nature, for both prophetic revelation and poetic inspiration come from the same source. Each, however, possesses a different degree of purity. Whereas revelation is regarded as immaculate and pure, poetic inspiration is often subject to corruption. Illustrating the hierarchial degrees of prophetic revelation as compared to poetic inspiration, in his *Treasury of Mysteries* Niẓāmī compares poets to prophets as follows:

> The veil of Mystery which is poetry
> Is but a shadow of the veil of prophecy.
> Amid the ranks of saints, the prophets take
> The row in front, then come the poets.
> In their vision (i.e. nature) both poet and prophet
> Of One Friend are confidants.
> These two are the heart and pith;
> The rest of men but crust and skin.[28]

Perhaps the most interesting metaphor used by the Sufi poets to indicate the ambivalent contact-point between the human and the Divine, between the human reedpipe's lip and the divine Musician's breath, which at the same time kept intact the transcendental nature of their poetic inspiration, is that of the parrot and the mirror. In mediæval times, in order to teach the parrot to speak a trainer would place a mirror before the bird and then sit behind the mirror and begin to speak. The parrot, imagining that the words he heard were coming from the other parrot it beheld in the mirror (rather than the human trainer behind it), could then successfully mimic the human voice. Using the same simile, the Sufi poets likened their heart to a mirror, on the face of which they heard the words which the divine Trainer instructed them to say. Just as the parrot in his speech merely mimicked the words of his human trainer, so the Sufi poet composed only those poems which the divine Inspirer vouchsafed to him. In Ḥāfiẓ's words:

> Behind the mirror I have been made to be like the parrot:
> I repeat what the Lord of pre-eternity has ordered me to say.[29]

4. The Fourfold Quest and the Role of Love in Sufi Aesthetics

We have observed above that love is aroused in the Sufi poet when he beholds beauty. Although this vision raises his perception to a higher realm, he still cannot resist the call to descend again into the realm of mortal perception to incite others to return to the realm of love and experience his vision.

Love in this context represents supreme human fulfillment. Having attained to love, the poet obtains the four perennial goals of the human quest:

i) the Philosopher's Stone of the Alchemists;
ii) the Panacea or Cure-all of disease;
iii) the Love-potion;
iv) the Elixir of Eternal Life.

References to the attainment through 'love' of these four perennial objects of desire pursued by man, recurs throughout all Persian Sufi poetry.

i) Defining love as alchemy, for instance, Ḥāfiẓ writes:

> Wash your hands of this base copper of existence
> Like the men of the spiritual Path

So that you will find the alchemy of Love
Which will turn you into gold.[30]

In the same vein, Rūmī incites the mystic to:

Set aside the copper of your 'self' like men;
Go to Love, reject base coins, until you become alchemy.[31]

ii) Rūmī describes Love as the panacea or cure-all of disease in the prologue of the *Mathnawī*:

Greetings, Love!
Joyous passion!
Physician of all our ills!
The cure for all our pride and conceit!
O You who are our Plato, our Galen![32]

iii) Concerning the perennial pursuit of the love-potion, Saʿdī assesses his own poetry as itself constituting a love-potion. Being the product of his intoxication, his verses will inebriate whoever reads them:

Learn loving-kindness from me
But should no life remain for me
Seek the mandrake root from my tomb.
Since from the clay of Saʿdī of Shiraz
The fragrance of love will be wafted
Even if a thousand years from now it's imbibed.[33]

A similar claim is advanced by Ḥāfiẓ concerning his own poetry:

Since you have accepted them
My words impress the heart.
Indeed, the discourse of Love
Leaves such a trace and mark.[34]

In fact, one sure sign of poetry inspired by love is that it is beloved by all, and in turn the only way to become 'beloved' is to be a lover, a lover of beauty.

iv) Finally, the elixir of eternal life is also love, since love is the key to youth. Describing his own spiritual state, Rūmī comments:

> I am not that kind of handsome youth
> Who tomorrow grows old and frail.[35]

Love not only preserves youth but turns the lover into a child, and for this reason, a certain childlike innocence and simplicity characterizes all of the great poets. In the words of Saʿdī:

> Whoever is close to you possesses all the fortune of youth
> He will never turn old since he dwells in seventh heaven.[36]

Exactly the same sentiment is expressed by Ḥāfiẓ:

> However old, heart-weary and incapable I become
> The moment I recall your face I become young.[37]

Or again:

> The heart of one quickened in love will never die:
> Our immortality is recorded in the tablet of the world.[38]

III. Poetic Metaphor: Form and Meaning

We have seen how the content, theme and meaning of Persian Sufi poetry is focused exclusively on divine Unity and love. The Persian theory of 'realism' shuns the minute depiction of all the diverse facets of nature as totally independent entities without reference to their transcendent whole; instead, it concentrates on the vision of the real

Being behind phenomena. In this sense, Sufi poetry follows what might be called a doctrine of 'absolute realism'!

Perhaps as a consequence of this radically metaphysical approach to nature, form (*sūrat*) has no independent significance of its own in Sufi aesthetic theory. Form is conceived of as the crystallization of the one meaning and theme, and considered for itself alone, is of minor importance. Hence, all Sufi poetry is to be taken symbolically rather than literally, and the great Sufi poets emphasize the essentially metaphorical nature of their verse. Sa'dī states this quite explicitly:

> O friends, close the eyes of your outward sensual vision
> For we have concealed certain hidden secrets behind these words
> If the whole world could behold the verbal form of my words
> None would ever be able to reveal their meanings.[39]

In a similar vein, Ḥāfiẓ states:

> These words I've written in such a manner
> That common man cannot understand;
> Peruse these words by the grace of your charismatic power
> In the manner you know is proper.[40]

Whereas in Western aesthetic theory, metaphor is divided into two parts: tenor and vehicle, in Sufi aesthetics, these two components are defined as *ma'nā* and *ṣūrat*, or meaning and form, with the latter acting as but a device to convey a higher meaning. For the 'formalist' writer, or non-mystical poet who strives to perfect his art using the vehicle of the metaphor alone, this becomes an end in itself, the tenor being only something superadded for the sake of exhibiting his or her skill and art.

For the Sufi poet, however, the tenor is *the creator* of the vehicle, and since the tenor comes from the world of beauty, the vehicle as *a consequence* is beautiful. Since the theme is sublime, the form is also sublime. This infusion of beauty into the tenor, as well as the vehicle, of poetic metaphor in Sufi poetry is best revealed in Rūmī's verse. Rūmī's verse embodies harmony, proportion, and balance—a veritable verbal music, whose forms dance in step with their meaning. Alluding to the aesthetic principle of the dominance of the tenor or meaning, over the vehicle or form, he wrote:

> The votaries of wine are all immersed in joy.
> Oh lovers of the corporeal sense
> All you hear is *do, re, me, fa.*[41]

Those who are concerned with the form of the poem alone, states Rūmī in this couplet, will merely hear the '*do, re, me, fa*' (*Tan-tan wa tan-tana*) of the Arabic musical notation but remain oblivious to the meaning. Correspondingly, Rūmī also states:

> Poetry is but a cloak of hair;
> Behold within who's hiding there:
> Either it is an angel lending lustre to the cloak
> Or a devil who strips you of what you wear.[42]

Yet despite the limitations of form, since form is a crystallization of the meaning, even the prosody of Sufi poetry is filled with music. Every classical Sufi poem is meant to be recited with intense rhythm and to be passionately sung with musical accompaniment. The poem's rhythm is made for *dancing* rather than academic learning or metrical analysis. Persian Sufi poetry is inseparable from song and dance.

IV. Beyond Wine and Glass: The Drunken Vision of Unity

Poetics and aesthetics in Sufi thought have an effect-cause relationship, insofar as the inherently refined feeling for beauty which the science of aesthetics presupposes, impregnates poetics with both formal and spiritual beauty. This relationship is illustrated by a poem which Rūmī once composed as an apology for writing a poem to which his master had objected.

I composed a poem while languishing for wine.
He (Shams) said: I expect better poems from you.
Fine, I said, but good poetry requires good wine.
Offer me your graceful gazelle, then take from me a ghazal.
Show me your radiant countenance like Sirius:
Then behold my fresh and lovely poetry.[43]

In these verses Rūmī's mention of the gazelle indicates the science of aesthetics without which good poetry cannot be composed; the 'ghazal-meaning' of the poem being reflected in its 'gazelle-form' and vice-versa.

I began this discourse with the wine of meaning, so must close it with the cup as a symbol of the form of poetry. While the poetic image of the 'wine of meaning' represents the simple and noncomposite divine Unity, the idea of the 'cup of form' is, on the contrary, a complex thing of utmost multiplicity. It is the cup which provides the diverse subjects of study which are collectively referred to as 'literary studies'—rhetoric, prosody, etc. Given the close relationship between music and Persian mystical poetry, a few brief comments on the science of prosody need to be made here.

The Persian metres are mostly derived from Arabic prosody which are based on quantitative rhythms organized according to orderly patterns of various combinations of short and long syllables. If studied in the traditional manner, using such texts as Rāzī's *al-Muʿjam*, this subject is highly complicated. However, the subject becomes much simpler, and even pleasant to learn, when approached through music. From a musical perspective, the metric feet can be simply divided into three kinds of musical beats: one, two and three. From this musical point of view, each group of feet is followed by one 'rest' corresponding to that group, which repeat themselves in various patterns. One particular pattern, for instance, into which a major portion of all Persian metres fall, is 1, 1, 2—with diverse permutations such as 2, 1, 1 and 1, 2, 1. The metre *par excellence* of much Sufi didactic verse, as well as much lyrical poetry, is the *Mathnawī*, which takes the following metrical form: 1, 2, 1 * 1, 2, 1 * 1, 2. Transliterated into Persian, it looks as follows:

Bish-naw az ney chūn hikāyat mīkunad /Az jidā-i-hā shikāyat mīkunad
1 2 1 * 1 2 1 * 1 2 1 2 1 1 2 1 1 2

The inspiration felt by the Sufi poet is primarily musical and rhythmical. That is to say, the poet senses the musical beat of the poem *before* composing it in a precise prosodic pattern, which constitutes the form of the poem, the spiritual 'cup' into which the 'meaning' is poured. Different spiritual moods or mystical states correspond to specific rhythms and metres expressed in various types of *allegro* (i.e. ecstatic) or *penseroso* (i.e. sober and grave) forms.

In this regard, one slowly comes to realize that in Persian literature, the cup and the wine are the one and same! Just as the body is inseparable from the soul, so the prosodic form or metrical 'cup' is one with the wine of inspiration and meaning. Just as ultimately every drop of water is itself the sea, the cup is also the same as the wine, for, in the words of 'Irāqī:

The wine is so pure
and the glass so clear—
One moment it seems
That all is wine
The next it all
The glass appears.[44]

NOTES

1. *Dīwān-i Ḥāfiẓ*, ed. Parwīz Nātil Khanlarī (Tehran: Sahāmī 'ām 1362 A.Hsh./1983; second ed.), ghazal 190, v. 6.

2. *Dīwān-i Ḥāfiẓ*, ed. Parwīz Nātil Khanlarī, p. 396, ghazal 20, v.1.

3. *Ṣamad Muwaḥḥid*, ed., *Majmū'a-i āthār-i Shaykh Maḥmūd Shabistarī* (Tehran: 1986) (Hereafter: MAS), *Gulshan-i rāz*, p. 101, v. 811.

4. *Dīwān-i Muḥammad Shīrīn Maghribī*, ed. Leonard Lewisohn (Tehran: Tehran

University Press; London: SOAS Publications, 1993), p. 19; VI: 1–4, translation by Leonard Lewisohn.

5. *Mathnawī-yi Yusūf va Zulaykhā*, in *Mathnawī-yi haft awrang-i Jāmī*, ed. Mudarris Gīlānī (Tehran: n.d.), p. 592.

6. *Dīwān-i Ḥāfiẓ*, ed. Khanlarī, ghazal 272: v. 4.

7. Ibid., ghazal 148, v. 1.

8. *Gulshan-i rāz*, in *Majmūʿa-i āthār-i ... Shabistarī*, p. 72, v. 139.

9. Sonnet 53, *Shakespeare's Sonnets*, ed. W.C. Ingram/T. Redpath (London: 1985), p. 123.

10. *Mathnawī*, ed. R.A. Nicholson, 8 vols. (London: 1925–40), Bk. VI, v. 1528.

11. Ibid., Bk. I, v. 498. (This verse is omitted from Nicholson's edition but follows I, v. 498 in most other editions.)

12. *Dīwān-i Ḥāfiẓ*, ed. Khanlarī, ghazal 40, v. 7.

13. *Shakespeare's Sonnets*, p. 177.

14. In this context, it might be said that the lyrics of Ḥafiẓ are the double-distilled brandy of Persian lyricism, expressing the sublimest aspects of the mystical bacchanalian tendencies of Persian poetry. Although all previous Persian and Arabic poets in one way or another communicate to us a certain degree of divine intoxication of Being in their poetry, thus raising our sights to a higher realm, Ḥafiẓ has adapted and distilled their inebriation twice over, making the purest poetic 'brandy' available in the Persian tongue.

15. *Gulshan-i rāz*, p. 101, v. 811.

16. *Kulliyāt-i Saʿdī*, ed. Hossein Muhyiddin Ghomshei (Tehran: 1996), in *Ghazaliyyāt*, s.v. *'bāqī'*.

17. *Ghazalhā-yi Saʿdī*, ed. Nūr Allāh Izadparast (Tehran: Dānish 1362 A.Hsh./1984), I, p. 120, v. 2.

18. *Dīwān-i Ḥāfiẓ*, ed. Khanlarī, ghazal 63, v. 4.

19. *Mathnawī*, ed. Nicholson, Bk. VI, v. 573.

20. This relationship between the madness of poetic inspiration and ordinary lunacy is also underlined by Plato. The true poet, Plato declares in the *Phaedrus* (545A), composes his fine poem not from art alone, but rather because he is inspired and possessed by the Muses:

> 'He who knocks at the gate of poetry untouched by the madness of the Muses, believing that art alone will make him an accomplished poet, will be denied access to the mysteries, and his sober compositions will be eclipsed by the creations of inspired madness.'

Most great Western poets and philosophers, from Socrates to George Santayana, from Homer to Emerson, have also acknowledged the truth of Plato's view about the 'selfless' and 'divinely lunatic' nature of poetic inspiration. In the same fashion, Sufis such as Rūmī profess that:

> My words lack charm whenever I am sober:
> Give me a cup or two when you ask me for a poem.

—*Kulliyāāt-i Shams yā Dīwān-i kabīr*, ed. Badī' al-Zamān Furūzānfar (Tehran: Amīr Kabīr, 1976), vol. 6, p. 132, no. 2835, v. 30101.

21. *Laylī vā Majnūn*, in *Kulliyāt-i Khamsa-yi Ḥakīm Niẓāmī* (Tehran: 1351 A.Hsh. /1972, 3rd. ed.), p. 452.
22. *Dīwān-i Ḥāfiẓ*, ed. Khanlarī, ghazal 119, v. 1.
23. *Mathnawī Yusūf and Zulaykhā*, in *Mathnawī-yi Haft Awrang-i Jāmī*, p. 578.
24. *Mathnawī*, ed. Nicholson, Bk. II, v. 691.
25. *The Koran Interpreted*, translation by A.J. Arberry (London: OUP, 1983).
26. *Mathnawī*, ed. Nicholson, Bk. IV, v. 2122.
27. *Mathnawī*, ed. Nicholson, Bk. I, v. 1936.
28. *Makhzan al-asrār*, ed. V. Dastgirdī (Tehran: Maṭba'a Armaghān 1313 A.Hsh. /1934), pp. 40–41.
29. *Dīwān-i Ḥāfiẓ*, ed. Khanlarī, ghazal 373, v. 2.
30. Ibid., ghazal 478, v. 3.
31. *Ghazaliyyāt-i Shams-i Tabrīzī*, ed. Manṣūr Mushfiq (Tehran: Bungāh-i Maṭba'ātī Ṣafī-'Alī-shāhī 1338 A.Hsh./ 1959, 3rd ed.), p. 600, v. 7.
32. *Mathnawī*, ed. Nicholson, Bk. I, vv. 23-4.
33. *Ghazalhā-yi Sa'dī*, ed. Izadparast, I, p. 12, v. 1.
34. *Dīwān-i Ḥāfiẓ*, ed. Khanlarī, ghazal 121, v.6.
35. *Kulliyāt-i Shams*, ed. Furūzānfar, IV, p. 46, ghazal no. 1705, v. 17843.
36. *Ghazalhā-yi Sa'dī*, ed. Izadparast, I, p. 109, v. 2.
37. *Dīwān-i Ḥāfiẓ*, ed. Khanlarī, p. 644, ghazal 314, v. 1.
38. Ibid., p. 38, ghazal 11, v. 4.
39. *Kulliyāt-i Sa'dī*, ed. M.'A. Furūghī (Tehran: n.d.), p. 634, vv. 8–9.
40. *Dīwān-i Ḥāfiẓ*, ed. Khanlarī, p. 644, ghazal 950, v. 4.
41. *Kulliyāt-i Shams*, ed. Furūzānfar, I, p. 300, ghazal 516, v. 5511.
42. Ibid., IV, p. 11 9, ghazal 1949, v. 20588.
43. Ibid., IV, p. 276, ghazal 2080, vv. 21958-10.
44. *Kulliyāt-i Fakhr al-Dīn 'Irāqī*, ed. S. Nafīsī (Tehran: 1959), p. 169.

Folio from the *Panj Ganj* (Five Treasures) of Jami (d. 1492), 16th century

The Symphony of Rūmī: Études in Rūmī's Poetry.

Prologue

In this chapter I will approach the poetic oeuvre of Rūmī as a grand symphony played entirely by a single instrument—the reed-flute (*ney*). I divide up the symphony into twelve different movements which together subsume the major themes of Rūmī's teachings. The various movements of this symphony, as will be shown, are constituted of certain recurring melodic themes, such as the unity of Being (*waḥdat al-wujūd*), freewill and predestination, love versus reason, philosophy and mysticism, the divine feminine, the soul's immortality, punishment and reward, and, of course, love (the most important movement that constitutes the keynote of the entire symphony), played to the harmonic accompaniment of memorable anecdotes, sage adages, and sweet tales.

More than any other Persian poet, Jalāl al-Dīn Rūmī's poetry is pervaded by ecstatic movement, filled with music, singing, dancing, foot-stamping, and hand-clapping. Gustav Mahler, the famous German composer, wrote a celebrated symphony known as the 'Symphony of a Thousand' because it requires a thousand musicians to perform it properly. Rūmī, on the other hand, for the sake of a single instrument, the reed-pipe or *ney* usually played by humble peasants, has composed thousands upon thousands of lyrical and didactic verses filled with points of philosophical wisdom, tales, and anecdotes, all of which are meant to be sung and set to music. In this respect, one could label his *Mathnawī* and *Dīvān-i Shams* together as a 'Symphony of the Sixty-thousands,' which is roughly the sum total of the verses in both collections. Whether the feet of his metres are arranged in *adagio* or *allegro* rhythms, the musicality of Rūmī's verse is permeated by a sweet concord, sustained by a spiritual ambience that expresses a self-perpetuating joyous harmony.

I. Prayer and Supplication

In the first movement of this symphony can be found a series of subtle mystical and romantic prayers and supplications with profound philosophical overtones. The following verses from the *Mathnawī* can be cited in this regard:

That place to the soul, God, won't you disclose
    Where speech without a word is born and grows,
So that the pure soul headlong will then race
    To non-existence's vast open space!
A wide and vast realm of magnificence
    From which this false world gains a sustenance.[1]

*

Teach us, Dear Friend, fine words that we can say
    To gain your mercy every time we pray!
Both prayers and their answers come from You,
    Security's from You and terror too.
If we have erred, correct ways please now teach!
    You're the Corrector and the Lord of Speech.
With alchemy you can transmute what's vile,
    Transform a stream of blood into the Nile;
Your work is to perform such alchemy:
    No one else knows this special chemistry.[2]

II. Poetry as Prophecy

Another movement of Rūmī's symphony relates to the prophetic dimension of poetry. It can be said that the message of Rūmī's poetry is 'prophetic' if we understand the term to refer to the prophetic faculty in the general rather than the particular sense. The 'prophetic' facet of Rūmī's achievement as a poet has been famously summed up by the celebrated Safavid Sufi poet and theologian Shaykh Bahā'ī (d. 1030/1621), who it is said composed the following verses in homage to Rūmī's *Mathnawī*:

That poem of the spirit,
  The *Mathnawī* of Rūmī,
Is all a holy writ,
  In Persian the Koran.
I won't profess that marvelous
  Colossus a prophet
But do confess
  His work's a sacred text.[3]

The *Mathnawī* itself is a deeply 'prophetic poem'. Its prophetic nature is addressed directly by the poet himself in various passages in different books of the poem. In the third book of the *Mathnawī*, for example, while telling the tale of the 'Mosque that Slew its Guests', Rūmī drops the thread of his story to contend with the cavilling of an asinine critic of the poem:

This yarn of mine has yet to end—yet look,
A putrid stench of smoke from envious folk
Flies up—a goose sticks out his head from his ass—
House's door, and railing like a bitch curses:
'This *Mathnawī* is vulgar verse, a shabby
Work of old prophets' tales, an idle fancy
That's got no talk of higher mysteries
Towards which careen the coursers of the saints,
Nor talk of stages of the Way—from self—

Restraint to annihilation of the self,
Ascent up step by step, each stage by stage:
Their *differentia* with commentary
Spelled out: the hows and whys of each degree
By means of which the heart's adepts fledge wings
And soar aloft to supernatural things.'
The pagans too lampooned the holy scripture
When it came down with such a caricature.[4]

Responding to his poem's critic, Rūmī compares his *Mathnawī* to the holy Koran, finding a similarity between the objections which critics assailed the Prophet with respect to the Koran and the dissent and hostility expressed by critics of the *Mathnawī*. The aspersions cast on the poem, Rūmī remonstrates, first strike the critic himself, showing up his poor judgment. Paraphrasing a verse of the Koran, Rūmī then justifies the verity of the inspiration of his own poem as follows:

God said, 'As 'simple' as it seems, the holy text
To you, then go and write a chapter up like it—
You *jinn*, you men and all you learned experts
Make it your task: write up but one such 'simple' verse.'[5]

The whole aim of Rūmī's work and his entire mission as a 'prophet' appears revealed in this same verse cited above by the critic of the Koran who had ridiculed—yet unknowingly complimented—the *Mathnawī* as being merely 'stories of the prophets and their followers'. Throughout all his works, Rūmī's struggle is to instill in his readers a faith in divine love, and to persuade—or, if you like, proselytize—people to follow the prophets in general and the seal of the prophets (Muḥammad) in particular. However, his understanding of the message of the prophets is an intensely interiorized one. His viewpoint is that of a dedicated esoterist. In the *Mathnawī*, instead of the dogmatic teaching of fanatical devotees of scriptures as they are recited by bigoted clerics who thump their holy texts and harangue crowds with sermons threatening damnation by fire and brimstone, Rūmī insists that the message of the Koran is meaningless unless approached and interpreted individually by each person, and appreciated through the faculty of spiritual taste or *heart-savour* (*dhawq*) based on their own unique apprehension and inspired consciousness:

> Which exegesis is correct?
> The one that warms you up,
> Which fills you up with hope,
> Ardour, stirs you to act,
> That makes you venerate, accord respect;
> But if it dulls your wits and makes
> You slack, that exegesis is perverse.
> God's word has come to warm you up and animate,
> To take the hopeless by the hands and make their heart
> Regenerate. The Koran's sense is clear enough.
> Go ask the text itself its inner sense and truth
> Or else entreat some burnt-out soul, whose passions are
> All ashes, who's lost his soul and self, laid down before
> The Koran limb and life, until he himself is
> The Koran in his vital spirit's deepest essence. [6]

III. Koranic Exegesis

Another 'movement' in Rūmī's heavenly symphony relates to his work as an exegete and commentator on the Koran and interpretation of all the various tales, legends, and visions that are found therein. Rūmī's knack at original esoteric exegesis (*ta'wīl*) of certain verses and passages of the Koran, considered as a book of Revelation in the widest sense of the word, is especially noteworthy. By the power of his poetic genius, the 'Islamic' scripture is transformed by Rūmī into a 'supra-Islamic' text of timelessly contemporary relevance, the ecumenical import of which concerns all humanity and is not confined exclusively to the community of Muslim believers. For instance, referring to a tale found originally in the Torah and the Old Testament,[7] but which reappears later in an altered form in the Koran,[8] the Prophet David, ostensibly known as one of the most notorious polygamists in human history, was said to have had ninety-nine wives, yet he still coveted someone else's wife. In the Koran, however, it is only mentioned that David coveted the one ewe of his neighbour, despite possessing ninety-nine of his own. The new turn which Rūmī's gives to this ancient parable is remarkable:

Although the sea's my throne, yet still I'd beg
To have a gulp of water from a jug.
If just like David ninety ewes belonged to me
I'd still covet to own my neighbour's only ewe.[9]

In Rūmī's exegesis, the Prophet David becomes a prophet of the Religion of Love, whose love is so all-inclusive as to leave no one outside the parameters of its ecumenical circle. Esoterically understood, David's love must be 'one hundred percent,' because to be content with any lesser—symbolically less comprehensive—love, would be merely 'ninety-nine percent'; hence, a heinous infidelity. As we can see here, Rūmī gives an entirely new twist to the excessive, insatiable lust of the over-sexed polygamous male. David's lust becomes interpreted as a kind of divine intoxication, his desire becomes a virtual religious requirement and essential injunction of the Religion of Love.[10]

In *eros* greed is glory, name and fame;
In other things, greed's inglorious shame.[11]

The Sufi cult of beauty decrees that Love be like understanding that grows bright gazing on many truths; Rūmī believes, like Shelley, that the heart that loves and the brain that contemplates but one object alone turns the wide world into a sepulchre.[12]

Another interesting aspect of Rūmī's work as an exegete of the Muslim missal is found in his very original interpretation of one of the most commonly cited verses of the Koran: 'Thee alone we worship; Thee alone we entreat for help' from the Opening Chapter (*Sūra al-Fātiḥa*, 1:5). In the following ghazal, we see how Rūmī provides his own original exegesis of this and one other verse from the Koran:

The lover's passion, drunken ways, intoxication
And youth and all such things arrived to become
Delightful Spring and make a close association.

They had no form and then in joy conceived some formal shape.
What's this? Just look, how subjects of imagination
Gained shape and form, a name and local habitation.

The heart is like a portal for the eye, for what
Comes in the heart then enters in the eye, and that
Becomes, without a doubt, recast in form and shape.

That's why the verse attests, 'the day that all hidden
Thoughts are divulged.' There's resurrection in the garden
When hearts expose the Chinese idol who all adore.

The message says, 'Take heart—a heart of courage, if
You've got a heart. How long will it remain eclipsed,
Your heart: befouled, besmeared by earthly grime and dust?'

Come wintertime the garden prays, 'Alone to you
We turn in worship.' Then springtime it prays anew:
'Alone to you, to you we turn in time of need.'

'To you we turn in worship' means: 'As supplicants
We've come, so open up the door to sweet delights;
Please do not leave us in distress, give us no grief.'

Their prayer, 'we turn to you in time of need' declares:
'My fruits are overripe and burst upon their boughs;
O Keeper! My branches snap! Don't let this be my lot![13]

IV. Prophetology

Prophetology constitutes yet another movement in Rūmī's grand symphony. Like Ibn 'Arabī in the *Fuṣūṣ al-ḥikam*, throughout his *Mathnawī* and the *Dīvān-i Shams* Rūmī constantly refers to prophets who appear in the Old Testament and Koran. However, unlike Ibn 'Arabī who laid special emphasis on one particular type of 'wisdom' that he perceived within each prophet, Rūmī underlines certain points of pre-eminence and distinctive types of subtle knowledge that each prophet incarnates. For instance, he speaks of the Prophet Abraham's (Ibrāhīm) station and particular characteristic as having expressed the idea of 'I love not things that set'—referring to Abraham's exclamation in the Koran after God displayed the kingdom of 'the heavens and the earth' to him. When in the darkness of the night Abraham beheld a star, he declared it to be his lord but once he saw it set, he despaired of it and turned to God Himself for guidance.[14]

For this reason, the spiritual characteristic manifested by Abraham according to Rūmī is his pure unconditional love of God without intermediaries. Abraham manifested the 'Station of divine Friendship' (*maqām-i Khalīlī*)—a love that is not content with anything less than God himself for friend and beloved—the traditional name for Abraham in Muslim sources in general and the Koran in particular being 'God's friend' (*Khalīlu'llāh*). As Rūmī explains in the *Mathnawī*, the transient shine of the stars of mortal beings and temporal objects of love become effaced before the light of the divine sun:

Lightning is transient, unreliable;
    You can't tell what lasts from what's temporal.
The lightning laughs—to ask 'At whom?' one might:
    It laughs at those devoted to its light.
Such light is flawed, unlike light which is best
    That which is far beyond the East and West:
Lightning we know *will take away men's sight*,[15]
    Eternal light though helps men in their plight.
. . . Abraham's soul one needs, to gain the light
    Which can, through flames, bring heaven to one's sight,

And to climb rung by rung up to the sun,
And not be stuck in this dominion.
Traverse the seventh heaven like God's Friend;
Say: *'I don't love the ones that set'*[16]—ascend![17]

In the following verses from the *Dīvān-i Shams*, Rūmī refers to the Koranic tale of the Prophet Jacob who mourned so much in separation from his son Joseph that his eyes turned white from weeping,[18] explaining that Jacob's paternal love for his boy was simply a foil for divine love.[19] He then refers back to the story of Abraham's spurning of transient 'things that set,' followed by the tale of Abraham's destruction of the idols worshipped by the Assyrians and his subsequent punishment by Nimrūd by being thrown into a burning furnace.[20] However, Nimrūd's fire seemed to him but a cool breeze, so that he remained unaffected by its flames which did not burn him because of his piety.

Jacob made his kingdom in the soul
Of midnight's windy flowing locks
To touch with just one kiss his boy's own curls
And face. The 'boy' was just an artifice
And God his aim, for as the Prophet is
My witness, there's no true lover smitten
With love for what's just human—man or woman.
For Jacob was of Abraham's own tribe:
'The stars that set'[21] and passing things for him
Were all in vain, and what 'declines' like nettles in
His eye. A friend like Abraham was all he could
Accept, none else, or else he'd not have thrown
His body headlong on the pyre's flames.[22]

If Abraham emerged unscathed from the flames of Nimrūd's furnace, it was because, in symbolic terms, the hellish fires of malefactors cannot affect God's saints. God's friends turn the entire environment around them into a garden flourishing with roses and sweet basil. This symbolism is expressed succinctly in one verse of the *Mathnawī* as follows:

> With Nimrūd in you, don't approach the flame,
> Become first Abraham to do the same.[23]

Another prophet frequently mentioned by Rūmī is Joseph (the Koranic Yūsuf).[24] Whereas Ibn 'Arabī conceives of Joseph in the *Fuṣūṣ al-ḥikam* as embodying what he calls the 'Wisdom of Light' (in respect to Joseph's insight into the spiritual degree of prophecy and the metaphysical imagination), in Rūmī's poetry Joseph is mainly viewed as a manifestation of divine beauty and grace. Rūmī sees the light and luminosity of Joseph's being as manifesting his interior beauty; in this respect he often uses Joseph as a symbol for divine Unity. Because all sovereignty, beauty, graciousness, wealth, and excellence are collected in Joseph's person one need not bring any other present for this Joseph, he remarks, than a mirror:

> What's the mirror of existence?
> Non-existence. Choose non-existence
> Then unless you're oblivious.
> Existence in non-existence
> One can make conspicuous:
> Hence men of riches lavish
> Their wealth on mendicants.[25]

Although Joseph is self-sufficient and needless in respect to worldly accoutrements and accomplishments, the one thing he does need is need itself—imploration and supplication—a teaching presented in Rūmī's *Discourses* as follows:

> A friend of Joseph of Egypt came to him from a far journey. Joseph asked, 'What present have you brought for me?' The friend replied, 'What is there that you do not possess and of which you are in need? But inasmuch as nothing exists more handsome than you, I have

brought a mirror so that every moment you may gaze in it upon your own face.'

What is there that God most High does not possess and of which He is in need? It is necessary to bring before God most High a heart mirror-bright, so He may see His own face in it. 'God looks not at your forms, nor at your deeds, but at your hearts.'[26]

V. Music and Dance (*Samā'*)

The most popular and charming aspect of—and certainly the most fascinating movement—in the entire symphony of Rūmī, is his praise of *samā'*, the Sufi concert involving the singing of mystical poetry accompanied by music and dance. In the opening two couplets from a famous ghazal devoted to *samā'*, Rūmī writes:

Samā'—what's that? From lords of mystery
A missive dispatched to us—for hearts in enmity,
A note from them of calm serenity.
The blossoms bud from wisdom
Winnowed in its pleasant breeze
And like a lovely chord, its plectrum strikes
    In Being perforation.[27]

Being exiles trapped in this sentient, terrestrial realm, as these verses expound, music brings us happy tidings from a higher, transcendental realm. What are these tidings and teachings? That man is not a tattered cloak upon a stick, not a paltry thing whose labours culminate merely in death and nothingness. No, that is not his final end—for ere long these bodily shackles will be rent apart and we shall be sent forth, returned to our genetrix who sent us here at first. The fact that we are borne aloft by music, transported unto the very borders of infinity where we may gaze through the aperture of music into eternity itself, is a sentiment constantly reiterated by Western poets and philosophers. Rūmī also finds the secret of music's delight to consist in contemplation of that musical pleasance where the ever-blossoming Garden of Love is in bloom:

> The music of *samāʿ* is like a window
> That lends access to your garden
> And on its sill to hear one note
> The lovers lay their ear and heart.
> That window is—alas—one grand veil,
> Although the veil's a sweet delight—
> Go, my noble friend and keep silent.[28]

Rūmī considers the entire mystery of music to stem from a faint recollection of certain celestial melodies and airs originally audited in paradise. Despite the fact that our faculties have since become darkened and dimmed by worldly preoccupations and the sensory attachments of the material realm, a memory of those heavenly tunes still exists in our unconscious. In that primordial paradise, we had originally audited those celestial melodies that flowed through our souls like a clear and limpid stream. Now, in this terrestrial exile all we can hear is the sound of a dreggy trickle of water gurgling down a black mudhole. Still, because of the love we still have for that primordial water, even such rustic tunes can send us into transports, causing us to become drowned in delight. Albeit, the delight bestowed by music on the material plane pales in comparison with that of the heavenly 'music of the spheres':

> The awesome din of drums, the bugle's hue and cry
> Appeared to him to be that cosmic trumpet's cry.
> From heaven's whirring spinning jenny we've received
> These tuneful strains and airs, philosophers thus believed.
> The circling gyres and the spheres' polyphony
> They maintained, gave men's voice and lutes this psalmody.
> Believers say those sounds came down from Paradise;
> Through Heaven's grace these shrill strains seem idyllic tunes.
> It was in Heaven we heard that dulcet measure
> For all of us were bits and parts of Adam there.

Although the dust and grime of doubt has left its stains,
A memory in us exists of those refrains,
Though now we're besmeared with earthly griefs and care,
Defiled, how should this bass and treble grant that cheer?
If water's mixed with piss and dung and excrement
It turns its nature to something tart and astringent,
Yet something of the nature of water remains
Therein, and though it be but piss, it kills the flames.
That's why, for lovers, song and verse and music is
Their food and drink, for there, their fancy finds focus,
There's concentration of the imagination,
One's inmost thoughts attain there invigoration;
In fact, by flute and horn find configuration.[29]

In some extraordinary verses from the *Dīvān-i Shams*, Rūmī likens music to '*Spiritus dei* of each and every thing—their whole reality' that gives 'shape to every reality of the cosmos,' as if music were a kind of abstract mathematics expressing the underlying realities of the universe through numbers and numerical relations:

Lover, mistress, soul-mate,
Your serenade, O sonorous ney,
  A heart-warmth inbreathes;
    Men's frostbitten speech you slay.
Your reed-pipe's hollow, void of fears,
So you relieve the heart of bonds and cares.
A master-draughtsman though unschooled and plain,
You sketch the likeness of each person's mistress.
Spiritus dei of each and every thing,
Their whole reality, you give shape to every reality
Of the cosmos. Which gamut fits your scale?
Lift up your head from the reed-pipe's belly:
This melody you play is lusciously savoury.[30]

For Rūmī, music is not simply an article of faith. It is religion and faith itself. Better than all the other fine arts, music attests to the transformation of inchoate plurality into unified wholeness. Because music's spiritual effect is holistic, effecting the transmutation of multiplicity into unity, Rūmī boldly announces that his religion—that is, his Muslim profession of faith in God and divine Unity—amounts to naught else but 'the science of music (*'ilm-i mūsīqī*)':

> O harp, I long to hear the tune of *Isfahan*.
> O flute, O ney, play me your burning, siren song.
> Go set the frets on *Hijaz* and sing me a sweet chorale—
> I am the bird of Solomon and long to hear his whistle.
> Bear him a gift of notes that range from *'Iraq* to *'Ushshaq*:
> I wish to hear the happy strains of *Rast* and *Busalik*.
> This melody demands you begin with *Husayni*.
> To tunes like *Zirkhurd* and *Zir-buzurg* I love to listen.
> This scale *Rahavi* put me asleep—enough!
> Strike up the *Camel-bell Song* tune—that's what I love!
> This science of music is the faith that I profess;
> On this I pin my faith, as God is my witness.[31]

Both in the *Mathnawī* or the *Dīvān-i Shams*, Rūmī's original poetic compositions are infused with musicality, melody, and rhythm. In the first place, he gives expression to his own thought which forms the intellectual substance and source of the internal melody of his poem. Secondly, he uses metaphors, allegories, parables, proverbs, and lovely tales to create harmony within the poem, thus adding fresh dimensions to his poetic symphony. Thirdly and lastly, when the intellectual and literary melody within the poem itself is recreated by means of the musical recital through the contemplative practice of listening (*samā'*) to his poem, an indescribable delight and pleasure is bequeathed the listener.

VI. Blind Imitation and Self-Realization

Another important movement of Rūmī's symphony concerns his polemic against the vice of blind imitation (*taqlīd*) as contrasted to his praise of the virtue of self-realization, known in Sufi terminology as 'direct experiential verification' (*taḥqīq*). Since religious conformism has been the source of man's error and corruption over the course of history, initially he states that one should not be a conformist (*muqallid*) because there is a world of difference between someone bound down by the manacles of religious precedent and someone who has directly and experientially realized a spiritual practice from within himself (*muḥaqqiq*). He maintains that anyone able to free themselves from blind imitation and have a direct experience of the reality of love will become utterly overwhelmed by the divine might and majesty. He illustrates this soul-shattering experience by telling the parable of the peasant who went into his stable in the dark and, thinking it was his domesticated ox, actually stroked the back of a wild lion:

A peasant tied his ox up one dark night;
    A lion came and ate it with one bite!
He came to see his ox, but had to look
    In every corner and each tiny nook,
And thus he felt the lion's legs and back,
    Its side and rear, but it did not attack.
The lion thought, 'If it was now more bright,
    His heart would melt, his stomach turn in fright.
For this he's stroking me courageously:
    He thinks that I'm his ox, since he can't see.'[32]

Following this anecdote, Rūmī makes the most direct statement in all his *œuvre* about the scourge of blind imitation versus the benefits of direct spiritual realization. He tells the tale of the Sufi who visited a dervish hospice (*khānaqāh*) during his travels, where he wished to stay for the night. The Sufi took his donkey to the hospice's stable, tied it up at a stall there, laboriously feeding his weary beast of burden with just the right amount of fodder and water. Then he went to join the dervish congregation, intending to enjoy the Sufis' company and musical concert. What he didn't realize was that these particular Sufis had no means of entertaining him. Being totally destitute and poverty-stricken, the Sufis, without informing their guest, had stolen and sold the traveller's donkey and then bought enough victuals to give their starving congregation a huge feast, which was followed by a huge concert in honour of their new guest. As the musicians and dervishes grew warm singing their devotional hymns, the vocalist suddenly began to chant: 'the ass has gone, the ass has gone' for the key choral song. The traveller surrendered himself to the spiritual ambience, happily chanting 'the ass has gone' alongside the dervishes, blindly imitating their conviviality, joining in their jubilation little understanding the coda that the duplicitous dervishes had concealed in their chant: that 'the ass has gone' was a secret threnody for his own forsaken mount!

The next morning when the wayfarer went to the steward of the Sufi congregation and demanded back his ass, he was told that the Sufis had stolen the beast and used it to buy victuals for the evening meal. 'And this you yourself must have known since you were singing, 'the ass has gone' all along with such deep religious fervour in the assembly. Although I tried to come and tell you several times what had happened, your ecstasy and engagement with the concert was so intense that I assumed you to be a true mystic content to be robbed of his possessions':

He said, 'I came so many times, I swear
To tell you about this sad affair,
But you were chanting with them, 'The ass has gone!'
With such great zeal, and then you went on and on!
I went back, thinking: 'He knows what occurred;
He's wise and still content though he has heard."
'They chanted happily,' the guest then said,
'The joy of chanting soon filled up my head.
I've been defeated through vile imitation—
May it be cursed with a complete damnation!'[33]

VII. Sense and Syntax

Another important musical movement in Rūmī's symphony concerns the correspondence between abstract ideas and their concrete expression in words, that is to say, the relationship between sense and syntax, a relationship roughly parallel to that of harmony to music. It is usually emphasized that in all his poetry, whether the mystical epic verse of his *Mathnawī* or the lyrics of his *Dīvān*, Mawlānā was not a wordsmith consciously preoccupied with polishing and refining the letter of his verse. While he evidently did not take much care to rework his poems word by word, it is clear that he was concerned that every line possessed proper verbal symmetry and lexical congruity as good poetry requires, expressed a harmonious balance of sense with syntax, that each couplet was couched in the right phrases, using precisely *le mot juste* to illustrate the ideas under discussion. Sublime ideas which enter the mind are just like melodies that come into a composer's head, and like those melodies these ideas bring along with themselves their own distinct rhythms, beats, and meters. For this reason it was not necessary for Rūmī to consciously take time out to ponder which rhyme and which meter to use in his poems, for as the inspiration of the *Mathnawī* descended, it came already 'in tune,' 'attuned' within the poet's mind with the sweet concord of song and music and meter, as he has in fact stated in those famous lines:

> I reflect and meditate on rhymes and meters.
> 'Only on me you should contemplate,' my mistress says.
> 'My rhyme-struck friend, relax,' she says: 'with me
> Here we'll rhyme in the meter of felicity.
> What's words, that they should ever occupy your mind?
> What's words? They're just the bristly hedge of the vineyard.'
> I'll go and sabotage all sounds and words and speech
> To spend devoid of these in loving you a single breath.[34]

In fact, for any artist who gains access to the fountainhead of poetic inspiration and creativity, the Muse herself automatically dictates the correct arrangement of the poem's rhyme and meter, and it is she who arranges the bouquet in which the rose of melody is set beside the sweet basil and green herbs of harmony. The following two couplets comprise some of the loveliest examples of the harmonious combination of ideational meaning (*ma'nā*) with its verbal expression (*lafẓ*), of sense with syntax, in all of Persian poetry:

In the fires of your hauteur and coquettish disdain
Go consume, commit to the flames the wares of our being,
For that subtle bequest's the lot of needy mendicants.[35]

*

I'm like the fabulous gryphon whose supplication
is just to soar above the whirligig of heaven;
I'm like the Lord of Fate, Captain of Destiny,
whose storm-troops charge and break the back of every army.[36]

VIII. The Eternal Feminine

One of the most important movements in Rūmī's symphony is composed in celebration of the topos of the Eternal Feminine.[37] During the historical period in which Rūmī flourished, women compared to men were confined to inferior social roles. An utterly absurd sexual apartheid prevailed that was maintained by the patriarchal establishment. Females were confined to their homes, kept in check and subject to a myriad of bigoted cultural mores and backward religious restrictions. Despite these unfavourable social conditions to which women were subject in mediæval Muslim Anatolia, Rūmī invariably glorifies the Eternal Feminine throughout the *Mathnawī*. He develops a conception of woman as a theophany which manages to break the mould of these primitive cultural mores. Throughout his poetry he celebrates the celestial degree of woman, praising her benevolent grace and all-encompassing beneficial influence on the lives of men. Rūmī views woman as a creature of hauteur, possessing the degree of the disdainful coquette. The degree of woman in Rūmī's view is properly that of coquettish disdain (*nāz*). She has all the hauteur of a heartthrob's ravishing loveliness (*maḥbūbiyāt*) and necessarily she attracts and allures man to herself by her flirtatious wiles and ways, so it is incumbent on her lover, if he be sensitive and wise, to secure her satisfaction and peace of mind.

The woman whose fair face enslaved the man,
    what happens when she starts to act the slave?
She whose magnificence will quake your heart—
    how will you be when she breaks down before you?
When hearts and souls are bleeding for her glances,
    how will it be when she's the one in need?
Her cruel tyranny has us entrapped—
    how will we plead when she gets up to plead?
'To men alluring'[38] as God fashioned things.
    how can they flee what God has made for them?
He made her that 'he might take comfort in her,'[39]
    so how can Adam now be cleaved from Eve?[40]

As both these verses and the revealed word of the Koran attest, the figure of woman is invariably rendered beautiful in the eyes of men. For this reason no man has ever lived who remained immune to woman's charms and winsome ways. Rūmī thus writes:

A Hamze and Rostam in bravery—
    His wife still keeps him bound in slavery,
Although his words could make the whole world sway,
    'Please redhead, speak to me!' he would say.[41]

Whether one is a mighty champion like Rustam, a doughty warrior like the Prophet's uncle, Ḥamzah ibn 'Abd al-Muṭṭalib, or the Prophet Muḥammad himself, whose revelation captivated and enthralled the entire world—but who yet, according to tradition, would continually ask his young wife 'Ā'ishah (a capricious coquettish redhead) to entertain him with her charming company and conversation—in the end Rūmī acknowledges that the man who is not in thrall to his wife or mistress simply does not exist.

Following the above lines in the *Mathnawī*, Rūmī strikes a lovely comparison in order to show the difference between the respective roles of men and women in society. The comparison he makes is universal in its relevance and suitable to every age, but the image is especially apt today as a lesson to women on how to preserve their desirability and love-worthiness.

> The water vanquishes the fire by shock,
>   but fire will make it boil up in the pot.
> And when a cauldron comes between the two,
>   it makes the water vanish in thin air.[42]
> Though outwardly above her you may tower,
>   you want her, so inwardly she has power.[43]

Here, Rūmī suggests we may liken man to water and woman to fire. Should nothing be placed in between them to serve as a curtain between the two sexes, the masculine water will certainly quench and extinguish the feminine fire without her fire heating up his water. If on the other hand, one totally segregates water from fire, the female fire will eventually peter out and end up as ashes without ever heating up the water. However, if one places fire and water side by side and juxtaposes a kettle between them, the water will not extinguish the fire while the fire will gradually heat up the water within the kettle and bring it to a boil. It is this ebullience that ultimately leads a man to seek a girl's hand in marriage, that drives him to set up a family, and that culminates in the warm congenial hospitality of their hearth and home, bestowing maximum blessings and felicity upon both man and woman.

If we put Rūmī's comparison into today's language, he is saying that man and woman have a psychological need to enjoy each other's company and become acquainted with each other's personality, characteristics, and virtues. Through continuous social contact they will better be able to properly understand their relation to each other. Men and women must not be segregated, rather taught to enjoy each other's company and companionship in various cultural, academic, and other social settings. A mutual longing between the sexes to live with one another will thereby be established, causing man and woman to achieve harmony between themselves, so that with open eyes they may learn how to be each other's mates and live together lovingly with one another.

Following these verses, Rūmī continues with the following lines penned in interpretation of a saying of the Prophet—'Verily women prevail over the wise, whereas ignorant men domineer over them.'

> The Prophet once said, 'Women all control
>   Intelligent men, those who have a soul,
> But stupid men rule women, for they're crude
>   And hold a simple, bullish attitude.'
> They lack all tenderness and can't be kind—
>   Their animal soul still controls their mind:
> Tenderness is a human quality,
>   While lust and rage show animality,
> A ray from God is the one you love,
>   Creative, uncreated, from above.[44]

In essence, woman is not a created being, Rūmī informs us in the last verse; she is herself, on the contrary, a virtual creator. She is a theophany—a ray of the divine. That ray transforms her into a semi-divine beloved, even if in truth our sole beloved be the Lord. In this respect, Jāmī's words bear citation:

> All loveliness that anywhere is manifest is his.
> It's him who's disguised behind the world's heartthrobs;
> He's there clandestine, pulling on the strings behind the scenes;
> His fate's decree makes every flirting tease to flaunt her charms.
> From him comes *joie de vivre* and love that animates the heart,
> Which slakes the soul and satiates the spirit and gives delight.
> All hearts enthralled in love with some chic *beau ideal*,
> Know it or not, love him in that seductive *femme fatale*.[45]

IX. Predestination and Freewill

Rūmī's power and profundity as a philosophical thinker is most in evidence in that movement of his grand poetic symphony where he raises knotty theological dilemmas and discusses abstruse mystical topics, issues which have embellished many a quarto with rhetorical flourishes penned by longwinded scholastic theologians over the centuries preceding him. He usually manages to resolve these difficult theological and theosophical issues by penning a single verse maxim or two—if, that is, one has ears to hear.

The relation between 'Predestination and Freewill' is one of those key issues that preoccupied Muslim scholastic theologians and which they debated endlessly but never managed to resolve in a satisfactory manner, since they invariably disagreed with each other's arguments, demonstrations, and conclusions. Thus Rūmī quipped:

> Till man's last day of resurrection
> debate goes on and on between
> Doom-men who teach predestination
> and partisans of free volition.[46]

In Rūmī's view, the advocates of freewill and predestination each have a valid case to make. Both positions are relatively right. On the one hand, it is entirely correct to say that everything is God's will and all has already been predestined by Him to occur. On the other, the feeling of freewill which we possess is also entirely in order, for each person is in hock to his own deeds and must inevitably reap the wheat he sows. According to the determinist point of view, in the words of Ḥāfiẓ:

> You'll free yourself of grief and heartache
> If you'd but hear this fine point of debate:
> You only give gnarling sorrow strength to bite
> If you seek for sustenance not of Providence.[47]

This determinist point of view is also expressed throughout the Koran, perhaps the most famous verses in this regard being:

> No affliction befalls in the earth
> or in yourselves, but it is in a
> Book, before We create it; that is
>   easy for God;
> that you may not grieve for what
> escapes you, nor rejoice in what has
> come to you; God loves not any man
> proud and boastful.[48] (Koran LVII:22)

As this verse reveals, all events occur according to God's will since all events and circumstances He has brought into being. The following quatrain (51) from Edward Fitzgerald's translation of 'Umar Khayyām's *Rubā'iyāt* gives one of the most beautiful summaries of the doctrine of predestination in all of world literature:

> The Moving Finger writes; and, having writ,
> Moves on: nor all thy Piety nor Wit
> Shall lure it back to cancel half a Line,
> Nor all thy Tears wash out a Word of it.

The apprehension that everything has already been predetermined from the very beginning of time by God can also be reconciled with the law of cause and effect insofar as every event has a cause, and then that cause another cause and so forth, until at last (since it is impossible to have a series of causes continuing back *ad infinitum*) one reaches the ultimate 'Cause of Causes.' Therefore, the source-spring of all those secondary causes and the originator of all events must be a First Cause, which is the Cause of Causes. However, insofar as the ways of Providence and the will of God are unknown to us, this apprehension of predestination in practice doesn't really affect our life as individuals or alter our interaction with one another in society. Furthermore, within ourselves we all clearly sense the existence of our individual volition and freewill, and according to the same law of cause and effect we also apprehend, for example, that if we ever wish to attain such and such an aim, we must act in a certain manner which is appropriate to its realization. Therefore each person has the distinct feeling within himself that he is responsible for his own actions and that others are equally responsible for their deeds as well.

In a satirical anecdote meant to mock a travesty of the high doctrine of predestination maintained by the philistine common man in order to justify his own knavery, Rūmī clarifies that the idea of predestination has no place in our daily lives. Whoever insists on emphasizing or giving prominence to the notion of God's compulsion in his secular affairs, he argues, should be subjected to punishment!

A man crept through an orchard in secret,
Climbed up a tree and tried to snatch some fruit.
The gardener came up and cried, 'You dog!
Stop, you thief! Don't you have the fear of God?'
'Chill out,' the bandit said, 'I'm but God's slave:
It's God who gave these dates to us, you knave!
You're so totally petty, so common;
It's wrong to scold me like a simpleton—
Uncharitably mean towards the Wealthy One.'

'Hey Joe!' The gardener said, 'Go and get
That length of rope for me. This man has got
A point, but first what he should hear about,
To get a taste of this debate, is what
Is called the 'stick,' or, 'brigand's riposte.'
The gardener's men then took him and lashed
Him foot and hand to that same tree. They thrashed
Him front and back, a shovel for their cudgel.
'Have you no fear of God? You're giving me hell!'
The thief protested, 'Have some shame, have sympathy!
It's agony! Where's your humanity?'

The gardener said: 'We're all but God's slaves.
This cudgel that we strike you with is God's

Own instrument. You're his bounden slave, us
The willing agents of His business.
The club is God's; its back and sides as well.
I'm but God's servant at His beck and call
Hitting you at His behest—that's God's will!'
The thief confessed, 'My fatalism was all
Amiss and false. I now repent of all
I said: Freewill is right! *Freewill! Freewill!*'[49]

All throughout the *Mathnawī* Rūmī makes frequent references to the advocates of both camps—freewill and predestination—the doctrines of each of which he carefully considers and deals with appropriately without favouring any one side over the other. His attitude towards this theological dilemma is best encapsulated by this adage ascribed to Abū Ja'far al-Ṣādiq (d. 148/765), 'Neither absolute determinism nor total freedom of the will exist, but rather something in between the two.' This saying implies that one should dismiss the idea that God ever imposes any circumstance upon a person through the direct force of His will. Nothing of the sort ever happens at all. Likewise, one should also discard the notion of the existence of any absolute freewill—that is, the false idea that man is somehow quintessentially able to determine his own destiny regardless of what happens throughout the rest of existence. In actual fact, the truth of the situation is all the occurrences that take place in the world do so according to God's will through the channel of man's freewill. Under no circumstances does God's will ever impede man from apprizing or having the conscious apprehension that his will is free and acknowledging that he himself alone is responsible for his own actions.[50] Hence, Rūmī comments:

The demonstration of God's compulsion
Appears in our distress and imploration.
It's human shame and awkwardness
That proves the truth of our free choice
For whence this shame if freewill's naught?
And whence this ruing and embarrassment?[51]

*

Human discretion and freewill has a clear proof
When you confess, 'Tomorrow I'll go do that or this.'[52]

The *Mathnawī* is full of many such theological discussions, as has been demonstrated with elaborate detail and erudition in Jalāl al-Dīn Huma'ī's two-volume work in Persian entitled: *Rūmī's Epistle: What does Rūmī Say?* (*Mawlawī-nāma: Mawlawī chi migūyad?*). Huma'ī's marvelous work features many lengthy discussions of a number of fascinating theological and mystical topics including the world's eternity versus temporality, continuous ideational renewal, substantial motion, the unity of the divine Essence, and the eternity of the spirit.

X. The Spirit

Regarding the eternity of the spirit, in particular, few poets can rival Rūmī in coining so many fresh and expressive metaphors, original allegories, and subtle images in order to enable the mind of man to apprehend the essence of the spirit and its immortality. According to Rūmī, in essence our being consists of an eternal, unborn, and uncreated spirit (*rūḥ*). The body, on the other hand, is but a child of—or rather a shadow cast down by—that spirit:

There is a bird in flight whose shadow has been cast
On earth, yet in the *mundus invisibilis* it
Flitters. Our body with its coarse, crass flesh is but
Its shadow—shadow of a shadow of the heart.
How should this body, this base physicality
Become its rank, be fit to know the heart's degree?
A man's asleep between the sheets and tossing in
His bedding, yet his spirit shines like heaven's sun.
His spirit's truant, sandwiched 'twixt the lining's wainscot,
His body's turning to and fro beneath the duvet.[53]

Speaking of the inspiration of the *Mathnawī*, he expresses the same idea as follows:

The wine fermenting craves our fermentation,
and heaven turning craves our understanding.
The wine got drunk on us, not we on it;
the body came from us, not we from it.
We're like the bee, the body's like the hive,
and like the hive each body's cell's constructed.[54]

The eternal spirit, a wayfarer condemned to wander in exile throughout this world, has descended into this terrestrial realm for providential purposes for a short space of time. The reasons for her passage through and presence upon the earth remain as mysterious and hidden as the sight of the spirit itself appears to the eyes. This spirit is a lovely girl vouchsafed to the intellect—which itself is endowed with an immense grandeur and nobility—to guard and protect. The intellect, her guardian, is tremendously jealous to preserve the girl's honour and so strives to conceal her behind a multitude of veils. Amongst these veils are the body itself which becurtains our soul, and our conversation and words that cloak conceptions and ideas. Indeed, how many words are spoken just for their own sake, intended merely to enthral a listener's ear and distract his eye from witnessing the spirit's beauty:

The Intellect is jealous of the Spirit's beauty,
That's why my poem overflows with allegory.
Why should Higher Reason of her be jealous?
The Spirit is already hidden quite enough—
The Intellect's light is the veil of her face.
From whom would you hide? Oh jealous one, your visage?

'I hide that Spirit even from myself,' Reason says,
'That's why this fleshly jealousy seems so intense.'

Like nightingales lament before the rose's face;
Distract her lovers lest they apprehend her fragrance.
Abstract their ear with rhetoric, with songs and speech;
Divert their minds from glancing at her countenance.[55]

XI. Death

The intellect, a spiritual subtlety, is the envy of the angels and the heavenly pleroma. Its residence here is but for a moment's breath and then it is gone, fled like a parrot from the cage of the body, flown back to the India of the spiritual world. Rūmī conceives of the physical frame of the body as being but a sepulchre, a tomb which every moment switches its location and moves from place to place. So it is incorrect to say we go down into the tomb upon death; on the contrary, when we die we finally gain freedom from the mausoleum of the body's physical frame. Referring to the idea that the divinely inspired voice of the saints can bring the forgetful human soul back to life, Rūmī writes:

From corpses souls ascend without a choice
Up from the body's tomb due to this voice,
Saying, 'This voice has a distinctive tone,
To grant life is the job of God alone.'[56]

According to another interpretation of death given by Rūmī, death is an awakening from being asleep in the midnight of the physical world:

Souls that are bound in bodies made of clay
Feel ecstasy when they can fly away,
They dance to songs of passionate, sacred love,
Expanding like the full moon high above.[57]

In another famous verse of the *Mathnawī*, he remarks:

Oh cannibal who've rent the pelts
of scores of Josephs,
Once from this leaden-legged sleep you wake
you'll be a wolf.[58]

There are numerous other images and interpretations of death found in his work, in which, for instance, death is compared to the resurrection of life at springtime, the exit of Joseph of the Spirit from the well of nature, or in which the terror of death is transformed into the delight of spiritual ecstasy.

XII. Love

However, the ever-recurring refrain of Rūmī's symphony is love. Like one of the underground rivers of paradise this theme courses beneath all of Rūmī's fruit-bearing trees of verse. If Rūmī's garden is continually flourishing and evergreen, it is because it is irrigated by that *aqua vita* which is *Eros*.

O God! O God!
Amor—encore! Amor—encore!
The love that we possess
Is dulcet, beatific, flawless.
Amor—encore! Amor—encore!
From love's aqua vitae comes our dance,
Not from the flute and not from ney and daf.
Deo gratias! Deo gratias![59]

He even begins an entire ghazal with the following invocation of the Water of Life of love:

Let the water of life of *Eros*
cascade through our veins;
That wine of midnight that we once drank
translate it into dawn tide wine. [60]

Rūmī views love as being the panacea of all pains:

Be joyful, love, our sweetest bliss is you,
Physician for all kinds of ailments too,
The cure for our conceit and stubborn pride
Like Plato here with Galen, side by side.

Through love the earthly form soars heavenward,
The mountain dances nimbly like a bird.[61]

Another of the qualities of love is that it is magical, acting as a love potion, so that anyone who imbibes the potion becomes beloved by everyone.

Regard each lover as beloved too
Since it depends on just your point of view.[62]

Love is also alchemy, transforming the base metal of the human soul into gold, elevating man to the loftiest degrees of humanity. Likewise, love is the elixir of life which grants immortality to everyone who is a lover.

Like true men set the base copper of your being aside:
Set copper aside and enter the elixir of existence.[63]

Love has also been likened to the keys of a closed door and the balm that soothes the aching heart:

Amor has got a ring of keys
dangling behind her as she walks.
All gates she opens with those keys
and each and every door unlocks.[64]

In another ghazal he writes:

I realized the origin of love
Was in a desert I stumbled on:
There lay unsullied limpidity
Free from all taint and impurity.
A thousand locks I saw there
Their latches wide as the heavens
Yet only a letter or two or three
Served as teeth for their keys.[65]

What else can be said of love? Whether characterized by metaphors referring to constant joy, eternal life, perpetual inebriation, or images of beautiful women or men, or cupbearers of wine, all goodness, blessings, joys, and delights in this world or the next are totally in hock to love. In sum, nothing of ultimate value—no virtuous accomplishment or work of art—can ever be achieved without love. All types of perfection that one would realize are conditional on love. Without love, neither religion, nor moral principles, nor faith, nor excellence, nor art, nor sincerity would exist, for without love all of these are but meaningless forms and shadows without any substance:

> Love is the substance and *prima materia*
> Of each thing of beauty one may fancy
> Although the forms and figures of phenomena
> Disguise the spirit through divine jealousy.[66]

As a *finale* to Rūmī's symphony in verse, I can do no better than offer a few verses in praise of love from several passages in book five of the *Mathnawī*, verses which, whenever they are read, sung, recited, or simply recalled have always seemed to me as though the glorious retinue of the Sultan of Love were passing before my eyes in all his glory and majesty:

> Love is a sea and heaven's vault, its foam and froth,
> Insatiable as Zulaykhā in love for Joseph.
> Love's rippling billows rouse the firmament to move.
> The world would all freeze without love's sultriness.
> Why would the mineral in vegetable life
> Efface itself, or plants to spiritual life
> Give way? Why else would Spirit into *pneuma* descend
> To fan the natal wind that made a virgin fecund?
> Each thing would lie languid as ice, frigid, listless.
> How could they fledge their wings and fly in swarms like locusts?
> Each flake of foam is a lover of Infinity
> That hastens upwards after honour, rank, and glory.[67]

*

In love whatever's heard or spoken has no place:
The ocean depths of love are fathomless.
No one can count the multiple drops of the sea.
The seven seas evaporate before love's sea.
It's love that makes the ocean boil like a kettle
And love that grinds a mountain into flint and gravel.
Love cleaves the vault of heaven with a myriad clefts:
What quakes the earth is but love's extravagance.
Muḥammad with true love in purity was weld:
'But for your love,' said God, 'I'd not have made the world.'
Because in love's affairs, Muḥammad was the best
And ultimate, he is elect amongst the prophets.[68]

NOTES

1. *Mathnawí*, ed. Nicholson, I, vv. 3092-94, trans. Jawid Mojaddedi, *The Masnavi: Book One* (Oxford: OUP, 2004), I, v. 3105-07 (corresponding to the Isti'lamī edition).
2. *Mathnawí*, ed. Nicholson, II, vv. 691-95, trans. Jawid Mojaddedi, *The Masnavi: Book Two* (Oxford: OUP, 2007), II, vv. 694-98 (corresponding to the Isti'lamī edition).
3. Translation by Leonard Lewisohn (L.L). The author of these extremely famous and oft-cited *Mathnawī* verses (often ascribed to either Shaykh Bahā'ī or Jāmī but found in the collected works of neither poet) in praise of Rūmī's *Mathnawī* is unknown.–Ed.
4. *The Mathnawí of Jalálu'ddín Rúmi, edited from the oldest manuscripts available with critical notes, translation, and commentary*, ed. R. A. Nicholson (London: Luzac, 1925-1940), III, vv. 4227, 4232-37, trans. LL.
5. *Mathnawí*, ed. Nicholson, III, vv. 4242-43, trans. LL.
6. *Mathnawí*, ed. Nicholson, V, vv. 3125-29, trans. LL.
7. II Samuel 11, 12.
8. Koran xxxviii:23-24. In the Koran, the story of David's murder of Uriah (by sending him into battle at a dangerous spot where he would certainly be killed), the husband of Bathsheba, whom he then made his own concubine (II Samuel 11) is not told, but rather the parable related to David by the prophet Nathan about the poor man's one

ewe taken by the wayfarer (II Samuel 12) to apprize David of his crime and bring home to him his sin. However, all the earliest Koran exegetes narrate the story of David's love of Bathsheba and his murder of Uriah as having been implied in these two verses.—Ed.

9. *Mathnawí*, ed. Nicholson, III, vv. 1953-54, trans. LL.

10. See 'The Principles of the Religion of Love in Classical Persian Poetry,' in L. Lewisohn (ed.), *Hafiz and the Religion of Love in Classical Persian Poetry* (London: I.B. Tauris, 2010), pp. 77-106.

11. *Mathnawí*, ed. Nicholson, III, v. 1955, trans. LL.

12. See Shelley's *Epipsychidion*, vv. 160-73.

13. *Kulliyāt-i Shams yā Dīwān-i kabīr az guftār-i Mawlānā Jalāl al-Dīn Muḥammad mashhūr bi Mawlawī, ba tasḥīḥāt wa ḥawwashī*, ed. Badī' al-Zamān Furūzānfar (Tehran: Sipihr, 1363 AHsh./1984), vol. 4, ghazal 2046, vv. 21574-81, trans. LL.

14. Koran vi:75-76.

15. Koran ii:20.

16. Koran vi:75-76, in reference to the statement of Abraham discussed above.

17. *Mathnawí*, ed. Nicholson, II, vv. 1542-45; 1557-59, trans. Jawid Mojaddedi, *The Masnavi: Book Two*, II, vv. 1546-49; 1561-63 (corresponding to the Isti'lamī edition).

18. Koran xii:84.

19. Confirmed in Koran xii:86.

20. Koran xxi:51-69.

21. See Koran vi:75-76. The Arabic verb afal is translated here as 'what declines' in the next line.—Ed.

22. *Kulliyāt-i Shams*, ed. Furūzānfar, ghazal 1035, vv. 10915-18, trans. LL.

23. *Mathnawí*, ed. Nicholson, I, v. 1606, trans. Jawid Mojaddedi, *The Masnavi: Book One*, I, v. 1617 (corresponding to the Isti'lamī edition).

24. For a detailed study of whom see Annemarie Schimmel, 'Yūsuf in Mawlānā Rūmī's Poetry,' in L. Lewisohn (ed.), *The Heritage of Sufism*, vol. II: *The Legacy of Mediæval Persian Sufism* (Oxford: Oneworld, 1999), pp. 45-59.

25. *Mathnawí*, ed. Nicholson, I: 3201-02, trans. LL.

26. *The Discourses of Rumi*, trans. A.J. Arberry (London: Curzon Press, 1993, reprint of the 1961 edition), p. 195. 'God looks not . . .' is a famous Prophetic tradition (*ḥadīth*). This story is also told in the *Mathnawī*, I, 3157ff.

27. *Kulliyāt-i Shams*, IV, ghazal 1734, p. 65, trans. LL.

28. *Kulliyāt-i Shams*, V, ghazal 2404, vv. 25392-93, trans. LL.

29. *Mathnawí*, ed. Nicholson, IV: 732-43, trans. LL.

30. *Kulliyāt-i Shams*, VI, ghazal 2994, vv. 31825-28, trans. LL.

31. *Kulliyāt-i Shams*, I, ghazal 457, vv. 4837-42, trans. LL.

32. *Mathnawí*, ed. Nicholson, II, vv. 503-07, trans. Jawid Mojaddedi, *The Masnavi: Book Two*, II, vv. 506-10 (corresponding to the Isti'lamī edition).

33. *Mathnawí*, ed. Nicholson, II, vv. 559-63, trans. J. Mojaddedi, *The Masnavi: Book Two*, II, vv. 562-66.

34. *Mathnawí*, ed. Nicholson, I, vv. 1727-30, trans. LL.

35. *Kulliyāt-i Shams*, I, ghazal 479, v. 5084, trans. LL.

36. *Kulliyāt-i Shams*, IV, ghazal 1633, v. 17105, trans. LL.

37. See also R.J.W. Austin, 'The Sophianic Feminine in the Work of Ibn 'Arabi and Rumi,' in L. Lewisohn (ed.), *The Heritage of Sufism*, vol. 2: *The Legacy of Mediæval Persian Sufism*, pp. 233-45.—Ed.

38. An allusion to the following passage in the Koran (III: 14): 'To men are made alluring and beautiful the joys that come from women and offspring, and stored-up heaps of gold and silver, and horses branded with their mark, and cattle and land. That is the comfort of the life of the world. But with God is the more excellent abode' (M. Pickthall trans., slightly modified).

39. An allusion to the following passage in the Koran (VII: 189): 'He it is who did create you from a single soul, and therefrom did make his mate that he might take comfort in her' (M. Pickthall trans., slightly modified).

40. *Mathnawí*, ed. Nicholson, I, vv. 2421-26, transl. Alan Williams, *Rumi, Spiritual Verses: The First Book of the Masnavi-ye Ma'navi* (London: Penguin Books, 2006), vv. 2430-37.

41. *Mathnawí*, ed. Nicholson, I, vv. 2427-38, trans. J. Mojaddedi, *The Masnavi: Book One*, II, vv. 2438-39 (corresponding to the Isti'lamī edition).

42. *Mathnawí*, ed. Nicholson, I, vv. 2429-31, trans. A. Williams, *Rumi, Spiritual Verses*, I, vv. 2440-42.

43. *Mathnawí*, ed. Nicholson, I, v. 2432, trans. J. Mojaddedi, *The Masnavi: Book One*, I, v. 2443.

44. *Mathnawí*, ed. Nicholson, I:2432-37, trans. J. Mojaddedi, *The Masnavi: Book One*, II, vv. 2444-49.

45. Jāmī, *Mathnawī-yi Yūsuf va Zulīkhā*, in *Mathnawī-yi Haft awrang*, ed. A'lākhān Afḍaḥzād, Ḥusayn Aḥmad Tarbiyat (Tehran: Nashr-i Mīrāth-i maktūb, 1378 A.Hsh./1999), vol. 2, p. 36, vv. 334-37, trans. LL.

46. Trans. LL. The version of the verse cited in the author's original Persian text that is translated here can be found in Jalāl al-Dīn Huma'ī, *Mawlawī-nāma: Mawlawī*

chi migūyad? (Tehran: Nashr-i Humā, 1385 A.Hsh./ 2006), I, p. 92. In Nicholson's (V:3214) and Isti'ilamī's editions (V:3216) of the *Mathnawī* the version of the verse is slightly different, being given as: *Ham-chinīn baḥth-ast tā ḥashr-i bashar/ dar miyān-i jabrī va ahl-i qadar.*

47. *Dīwān-i Khwāja Shams al-Dīn Muḥammad Ḥāfiẓ*, ed. Parvīz Nātil Khānlarī (Tehran: Intishārāt-i Khawārazmī, 1359 A.Hsh./1980), ghazal 472:1, trans. LL.

48. *Koran*, trans. A.J. Arberry (Oxford: OUP, 1982), LVII:22.

49. *Mathnawí*, ed. Nicholson, V:3077–86, trans. LL.

50. For further discussion see Huma'ī, *Mawlawī-nāma*, I, pp. 81–83; and *Mathnawí*, ed. Nicholson, V:3022ff.—ED.

51. *Mathnawí*, ed. Nicholson, I:618–19, trans. LL.

52. *Mathnawí*, ed. Nicholson, V:3024, trans. LL.

53. *Mathnawí*, ed. Nicholson, VI:3306-08, trans. LL.

54. *Mathnawí*, ed. Nicholson, I:1811-13, trans. Alan Williams, *Rumi: Spiritual Verses*, vv. 1821-23.

55. *Mathnawí*, ed. Nicholson, VI:688-90, 693, 700-01, trans. LL.

56. *Mathnawí*, ed. Nicholson, I:1931-32, trans. J. Mojaddedi, *The Masnavi: Book One*, vv. 1941-42.

57. *Mathnawí*, ed. Nicholson, I:1346-47; trans. J. Mojaddedi, *The Masnavi: Book One*, vv. 1355-56.

58. *Mathnawí*, ed. Nicholson, IV:3662, trans. LL.

59. *Kulliyāt-i Shams*, I, ghazal 94, vv. 1044-45, trans. LL.

60. *Kulliyāt-i Shams*, IV, ghazal 1821, v. 19109, trans. LL.

61. *Mathnawí*, ed. Nicholson, I, v. 23-25, trans. J. Mojaddedi, *The Masnavi: Book One*, I, vv. 23-25.

62. *Mathnawí*, ed. Nicholson, I, v. 1740, trans. J. Mojaddedi, *The Masnavi: Book One*, I, v. 1750.

63. This verse (*mis-i khwud rā bih yik sū nih chūn mardān // gudhār az qalb u dar iksīr mīraw*) is absent from both the Furūzānfar or Subḥānī editions of the *Kulliyāt-i Shams* but can be found in some unpublished Indian manuscripts of the Dīvān.

64. *Kulliyāt-i Shams*, V, ghazal 2336, v. 24728, trans. LL.

65. *Kulliyāt-i Shams*, II, ghazal 583, v. 6176, trans. LL.

66. *Kulliyāt-i Shams*, II, ghazal 1012, v. 10680, trans. LL.

67. *Mathnawí*, ed. Nicholson, V, vv. 3853-58, trans. LL.

68. *Mathnawí*, ed. Nicholson, V, vv. 2731-32, 2735-38, trans. LL.

‘The hoopoe addresses the assembled birds’, folio 11r from *Mantiq al-tayr* (The Conference of the Birds), of Farid al-Din ‘Aṭṭār, painted by Habiballah of Sava, *ca.* 1600

Of Scent and Sweetness: ‘Aṭṭār and his Legacy in Rūmī, Shabistarī and Ḥafiẓ[1]

In this mall full of perfume shops, where women try
The fragrant scents, Each sort and brand, savouring each ware,
Don't gad about, but go sit down in the stall of one
Who sells the luscious sweetness there.

—Rūmī[2]

‘Aṭṭār the poet was as the Spirit;
Sanā‘ī the sight of both its eyes.
Our precedent we take
From both those poets:
We walk Sanā‘ī's path,
We tread in ‘Aṭṭār's steps.

—Rūmī[3]

Exordium

‘Aṭṭār remains the supreme raconteur in the sacred oratory of the Persian Sufi tradition. Like Shahrzād, the famous heroine of the Arabian Nights, he keeps the candle of the lovers' night-vigil lit with his colourful tales and sweet verses, lest wayfarers on the path of love journeying through the dark night of the world succumb to slumber. First, he ensnares and enchants us by his verse, after which he sets us to work grooming and combing apart the tangled ringlets of the curls of the pre-eternal Beloved—She who is at once all seven levels, or seven cities, or seven valleys, of Love—an enchantress who possesses all the lore of the divine mysteries, the mistress of Sufi gnosis. The enchantment evoked by the recital of ʿAṭṭār's poetry finds its perfect reprise in the opening invocation of Ḥāfiẓ's famous ghazal:

Friends come and let's unbind
The tangled curls of the Friend.
The night promises to be sweet—
With this romance let's make it last.[4]

ʿAṭṭār flourished in a day and age in which the Mongols drenched the earth with the blood of millions of innocent victims throughout the province of Khurāsān. Although his blood was also spilled on the earth at their hands, he himself paid the blood-price for his murder, drop by drop, verse by verse, offering us the wondrous spiritual musk of the Mongolian gazelle from his pen:

O ʿAṭṭār, in every line of your verse
  A fragrance like the musk-gazelle's navel
    Which you disperse upon the world
      Reveals a myriad mysteries' largesse.
Your poetry impassions the world's lovers
  Inconstant forever with skittish fervour;
    A whiff of your verse makes redolent
      The whole world with spice and scent.[5]

The same sweet fragrance of love whose celestial odour and heavenly aroma ʿAṭṭār here *implicitly* evokes also indues his verse with this same scent of musk:

You've caused a secret
Moon to hide Inside a little pod of musk—
Then made the musk itself distraught,
Caught in shafts of lunar light.[6]

*

The fragrance of your heavy tress
Has filled the world with loveliness.
Alas! You set yourself all at once
Aside and then vacate your place.
The fragrance of your musky hair
Whose scent the breeze bears everywhere
Has thrown up out a delirious gurgle
Beneath the restless ocean of the world.[7]

The same fragrance of the mystical musk again is *explicitly* evoked by Rūmī in this verse in which he advises and admonishes us about its most efficacious use:

Don't rub this musk upon your flesh and face—
Anoint the heart with it instead.
What's that musk? The Name
Most pure, of Majesty sublime.[8]

ʿAṭṭār is the leader of every spiritual company dedicated to the diffusion and olfaction of this Sufi musk, whose fragrance intoxicated the hearts and minds of those who sat in the circle of love which was later formed by Rūmī, Saʿdī, Shabistarī, and Jāmī. In the Persian Sufi poetical canon, ʿAṭṭār remains the chief perfumer and his wild, ever redolent scent, throbs and stirs the soul throughout Ḥāfiẓ's verse:

Press your kiss on the lip of the cup;
And then let drunkards drink up a sip.
With this gesture of grace and elegance
Revive the hearts of all your friends.[9]

Although the perfume purveyed by ʿAṭṭār hails geographically from Persia, when wafted into the West today, it still conveys the same pungent scent, quickening effect and the same celestial fragrance of spiritual musk indued with the perfume of divine Love, which the greatest of the Arab Sufi poets, Ibn Fāriḍ, evokes in this couplet:

If the fragrance of this wine were wafted once from
the East to the West,
So those whose sense of smell had died were graced by it,
A whiff of it would revive and cure all loss of sense.[10]

And yet 'Aṭṭār-the-perfumer was not the first entrepreneur to make a literary sensation in the Sufi perfume market. His verse had many illustrious forebears in the canon of Persian poetry, including the likes of Firdawsī, Sanā'ī, Niẓāmī and even Nāsir-i Khusraw. Albeit neither Firdawsī nor Nāsir-i Khusraw were mystics in any normative sense of the word, yet all these poets who preceded him, mystics or not, scented him with the incense of their passionate rhyme and reason so that his every word literally reeks with the musk of their eloquence. From all these perfumers in the bazaar of love, hawking the wares of their marvellous diction, 'Aṭṭār adopted whatever he could, following the scented trail of their sweet verse, setting out large cakes of sugar, diverse varieties of sweetmeats and confectionery on the tablecloth of his epic and lyric poetry to entertain us—his guests.

And yet, whatever he took in the way of ideas and expressions from them—which our dear literary critics confidently announce to be his 'borrowings and influences'—did not comprise mere imitative phrases, mimed and rhymed tropes, nor for that matter, smartly coined, clever turns of speech. In this sense, the following verse by Maḥmūd Shabistarī, frankly acknowledging the 'influence' of 'Aṭṭār upon his own great poem—*The Garden of Mystery*—rings equally true of 'Aṭṭār's poetic oeuvre vis-à-vis his illustrious forebears:

My verse is made by hazard and not design;
I'm not a demon who's tapped an angel's line.[11]

The principal capital and main source-spring of inspiration which any poet draws upon is personal experience. 'Aṭṭār, being a poet on a grand scale, expresses not just experience drawn from the understanding and the senses, but his personal spiritual realization. 'Aṭṭār's poetry is thus 'the fruit of direct certitude', as Rūmī described his own verse, and 'not merely a matter of argumentative demonstration or imitation'. After the death of 'Aṭṭār (d. 618/1221 or 627/1229) one can find very few poets in the Persian language who had not, in one way or another, utterly succumbed to the influence of his style. Among the vast troupe of his followers and imitators, however, three particular poets stand out. These are, in chronological order: Jalāl al-Dīn Rūmī (d. 1273), Maḥmūd Shabistarī (d. after 1340), and Ḥāfiẓ (d. c.1389).

I. 'Aṭṭār's Scent in Rūmī's Verse

Rūmī's verse is steeped more deeply in the fragrance of 'Aṭṭār's poetry than either of the last-mentioned authors. His *Mathnawī*, which is the natural continuation of the *mathnawī*s of 'Aṭṭār, represents the high point of all the previous Persian Sufi epics that began with the *Ḥadīqat al-ḥaqīqa* of Sanā'ī, and was then expanded and elaborated upon in 'Aṭṭār's *Manṭiq al-ṭayr* and other *mathnawī*s. 'Aṭṭār's main *mathnawī*s—that is, the *Asrār-nāma*, the *Ilāhī-nāma*, the *Muṣībat-nāma*, and, more important than these, the *Manṭiq al-ṭayr*—set down the firm foundations upon which the towering structure of Rūmī's monumental edifice, the *Mathnawī*, was later erected. To this influence, Rūmī's verse, cited in the epigraph of this essay, bears ample witness:

> 'Aṭṭār the poet was as the Spirit;
> Sanā'ī the sight of both its eyes.
> Our precedent we take
> From both those poets:
> We walk Sanā'ī's path,
> We tread in 'Aṭṭār's steps.

'Aṭṭār was 'the Spirit', since his words evoked the grand spiritual revival of the Persian Sufi tradition. His verse was like the breath of the Messiah, resurrecting the dead stranded in the veil of passion, quickening them, giving them new life, guiding them through the seven valleys of love. Sanā'ī represented 'both eyes' of spiritual insight, which contemplated the higher realm of wisdom and gnosis from whose heights the Sage of Ghazna divulged so many of the divine realities.

Rūmī, like ʿAṭṭār, was also an expert raconteur in the assembly of mystical adepts. But besides being a master of the mysteries of intuitive spiritual taste (*dhawq*) and a supreme poet-storyteller, Rūmī had a higher didactic aim in setting forth the *dicta* and *exempla* of the Sufis. By setting the snare and baiting it, he intended to catch us fowls fortunate enough to catch a whiff of the bait—which is nothing less than his deep contemplative experiences, his meditative reflections, his mystical insights and states. The snare which he set was aimed not at entrapment but was directed at our emancipation and realization of a higher consciousness. As such, the elements of ecstasy, intoxication, passion and, in general, mystical awareness, are more strongly evoked and evinced in the work of Rūmī than that of ʿAṭṭār. Rūmī's flights of poetic imagination are far loftier, the eloquence of his poetic expression more refined and sophisticated than that of ʿAṭṭār. ʿAṭṭār always keeps a tight grip on the reins of speech. His particular style of verse is sober: he proceeds methodically, step by step. In this respect, his ability to preserve a story line and hold together the unity of the narrative is simply inimitable. Having finished a story, he rounds it off with a moral, before returning to further disquisition on the Sufi teachings relating to that moral. In contrast, Rūmī appears mounted on a wild colt, gripping the reins of speech more loosely, so that he seems to let the steed of his verse gallop on of its own accord. Often he lets the reins of his discourse—the thread of his story—drop from his hand entirely. Taking flight on the Pegasus of his own transcendent inspiration, he soars into the heavens of higher imagination and understanding, whence he brings back for us—plodding pedestrian wayfarers—strange spiritual insights full of subtle, celestial modes of thought. When from that Empyrean he finally descends to tread alongside us common mortals upon the face of the earth again, he picks up the reins and resumes the thread of his tale.[12]

Setting these differences in literary style and mystical expression between the two poets aside, the *Mathnawī* of Rūmī lies, as was mentioned above, directly in the natural tradition of the *mathnawī*s of ʿAṭṭār. Most of the time, Rūmī's verse appears as the proper culmination of the Sufi epics of ʿAṭṭār. The literary continuity between the two poets becomes more evident when one considers just how many stories and various mystical allegories Rūmī adopted directly from ʿAṭṭār's *Memoirs of the Saints*. Although Rūmī often seems to be more successful in the art of story-telling and in the process of adducing a moral to a tale, the discourse of ʿAṭṭār has its own unique flavour and fragrance. Thus one cannot simply discard the *mathnawī*s of ʿAṭṭār and replace them with the 'spiritual couplets' of Rūmī. In fact, it might even be said that the mystical, detached and spontaneous humour of ʿAṭṭār in respect to the exposition of spiritual truths in certain instances, excels even the highest flights of Rūmī. The following verses from various *mathnawī*s of ʿAṭṭār amply prove this:

What man knows
    what's worth more
in this deep sea—
    pebbles of sand,
or coral cornelian.[13] [carnelian]

*

Not a soul is left alive in all
the long caravan, just so the craw
of a crow be kept well fed and full.[14]

*

A hundred thousand infants' heads
were lopped off from the neck
So Moses in the seer's inward sight
might just once become adept.[15]

Likewise, this sublime invocation, with its inimitable passion and exceptional originality, could never have been uttered by anyone other than ʿAṭṭār:

Give me an ounce of pain,
O You who cure all pain, for left without

Your pain, my soul will die.
To heretics let heresy apply,
And to the faithful—grant them faith;
But for the heart of ʿAṭṭār, let
One ounce of your pain remain.[16]

Such inimitable maxims minted in verse occur by no means infrequently in the works of ʿAṭṭār. His 'high art' of storytelling and his theatrical presentation of the frame-story's key themes and of moral points couched in peerless poetic aphorisms easily enables the reader to rend the veils of spiritual heedlessness. *In this particular aspect*, ʿAṭṭār excels even Rūmī!

But detecting and exposing the particular *scent* of ʿAṭṭār's language within the poetic *dicta* of Rūmī is well beyond the scope of any single essay. Only a full monograph could do such a theme justice. Here, the presence of ʿAṭṭār in Rūmī's *Mathnawī* can only be given by way of certain brief indications. A Nishapurian fragrance is sometimes directly imbibed from the verse of our Master of Konya, as in the first book of the *Mathnawī*, where Rūmī inserts a verse of ʿAṭṭār in the prose caption heading his story to illustrate the topic he wishes to expound, using ʿAṭṭār as a 'proof-text' to help state and make his point.

O soul that's lapsed and bound in ignorance
You know not what you are, so roll and chafe
In dust and blood, and fret to death with grief:
That's but your fate. And yet to heart-adepts
Sweet are the uses of adversity—though poisonous,
To them the hemlock tastes sweet and luscious.[17]

Rūmī renders a lengthy exposition on this one couplet of ʿAṭṭār's in twelve couplets of his own, two of which are as follows

Since in you the tyrant Nimrod lurks
Don't take a step into fire. Become first
Like Abraham, hid safe within the furnace.
Don't take a leap in pride and arrogance

Out in the sea, since you're no sailor nor
Good swimmer. When men who are inferior
Get gold in hand, it turns at once to dust
But perfect men turn earth into gold-dust.[18]

How thoroughly Rūmī's verse is steeped in 'Aṭṭār's is obvious to anyone attuned to the diction of the two poets. Although Rūmī rarely mentions 'Aṭṭār by name as he does here, wherever he does it is always with the utmost veneration. While no doubt he considered it redundant to cite the source of his inspiration for each verse in every case or explicitly state that this or that line or image was adapted from his Nishapurian forebear, the earlier poet's all-pervasive influence on him he directly acknowledged in the following oft-cited verse:

'Rūmī' is my name, from
Whence I'm known as
The 'Prince of Rum',
Although from all my verse
A luscious sweetness pours—
    In rhetoric and *belles lettres*
    To 'Aṭṭār I'm a slave.[19]

Numerous instances can be found throughout the *Mathnawī* where Rūmī has adapted tales from 'Aṭṭār's epic poems and recreated them in his own language. Sometimes he keeps the very same moral but retells the parable; other times, he changes the moral to suit his own particular exposition. By way of demonstrating both the similarities and the differences with regard to the two poets' varying narrative styles and modes of mystical interpretation of Sufi stories, the following tale, where 'Aṭṭār recounts the story of the mouse who seized the reins of a camel and ran off dragging the camel behind him, may be cited:

> Once I heard that a mouse in the desert came across a lost camel. So he seized the camel's reins and ran off, letting the camel follow docilely behind. The mouse soon brought the camel to its home, which was a hole in the ground. Of course, there was no room for the camel

down there. So the mouse turned to the camel and said, 'Well, it seems you have lost your way: I have found my home. Where is yours?'[20]

In the second book of the *Mathnawī* (v. 3436-3438) Rūmī retells this tale, but gives it a very different moral:

> A little mouse seized the reins of a big camel. It scampered off audaciously, dragging the reins of the beast behind it. From the camel's alacrity in following it, the mouse swelled with pride, thinking itself a champion. The clairvoyant camel saw right through the mouse's fantasy and hummed to itself, 'Just go on happily; I'll show you yet'.[21]

Although the essential message of both stories is similar, from the narrative point of view the recital of this tale in the *Mathnawī* is different in respect to almost every detail. The moral is simple: each person should take care not to transgress beyond his or her own limitations; the sincere seeker should always take care to preserve moral proprieties and maintain the prerequisites of his own spiritual and social condition, just as the Tradition of the Prophet teaches: 'Bliss is reserved for the one who comprehends his own limitations and does not overstep them.'

Rūmī also adopts and reinterprets the tale of the old harpist that was originally told by 'Aṭṭār in the *Muṣībat-nāma*.[22] 'Aṭṭār relates that an aged musician had lost all his admirers, fans and generous patrons who had hitherto been willing to support him. Finding no one interested any longer in paying him to strike up a tune, he went to a mosque, where he entreated God: 'O Lord, for Your sake alone do I now pluck my harp. So it is You Who must pay me'. At that very moment it happened that a disciple of the great Sufi saint Abū Sa'īd Abū'l-Khayr (357/967–440/1048) sent a charity offering of one hundred dinars to the saint. Although Abū Sa'īd's disciples coveted the money for the expenses of their hospice, with his powers of clairvoyance, the saint ordered that the alms be distributed to the destitute musician who had taken refuge in the mosque.[23]

In Rūmī's narration of this story in the *Mathnawī*, he expounds a number of subtle philosophical and theosophical points not found in ʿAṭṭār's tale. He describes, for instance, the effect of music on the human spirit, soul, and the saints, and even discusses such matters as the manner in which the Day of Judgment will occur. He raises many other issues as well which give his account of the story a deeper philosophical edge than is found in ʿAṭṭār's narration of the tale. Historically, he transposes the story back five centuries earlier, making it refer to the reign of the Caliph ʿUmar in the seventh century instead of Abū Saʿīd who flourished four centuries later.

Similarly, Rūmī retells (*Mathnawī* 5) the tale of Ayāz, the favourite slave of Maḥmūd of Ghazna, that was first recounted in Persian verse by ʿAṭṭār in the *Muṣībat-nāma*.[24] He preserves ʿAṭṭār's basic narrative structure but elaborates and ornaments the tale in his own unique, colourful way.

As Rūmī relates, legend has it that Sulṭān Maḥmūd put a priceless pearl (or, in ʿAṭṭār's account, a precious ruby goblet) into the hand of his chief vizier and ordered him to smash it to pieces. Instead of immediately obeying the order, the vizier smartly exclaimed, 'What a pity to break such a priceless pearl!' In turn, the sultan presented the same pearl to various other courtiers in his audience chamber. Feigning deference to his will, they all answered him in the same vein, taking their cue from the vizier, and politely protesting the irrationality of the king's direct command. In this fashion, the pearl was bandied about the room and passed from hand to hand amongst the courtiers, but none found the courage within themselves to smash the priceless stone. At last, the precious pearl landed in the palm of the sultan's favourite slave Ayāz, who straightaway picked up a stone and smashed it to pieces. Heaving a collective sigh of regret, everyone in the room turned on him and demanded, 'How could you have been so senseless as to have broken the sultan's priceless, unique gem?'

'Indeed', replied Ayāz, 'I smashed the pearl, but you shattered the precious stone of the king's command—and that is of far dearer, far greater worth.'

In both poets' account of the tale, the sultan is symbolic of God, while Ayāz the slave represents the true lover of God.

Besides the foregoing tale, there is the story of Ayāz and his old sheepskin coat, first recounted by ʿAṭṭār in the *Muṣībat-nāma*,[25] which

Rūmī recounts and redesigns in his *Mathnawī*. Rūmī displays special skill in his narration of this tale, to which he devotes great attention. In fact, wherever this story crops up in Rūmī's work, the author is always transported into ecstasy—to use his own metaphor: 'His elephant recalls the land of India'. He lets the reins of his narrative drop, being transported in rapture to the realm of higher spiritual mysteries. So profound is the impact of the tale on him that in one passage he remarks, 'I've become a lunatic now and have lost the whole thread of the story of Maḥmūd of Ghazna and the sublime character of his slave Ayāz.'[26] Then, he continues, 'Ayāz has become as thin as a hair out of love for you. I have lost the thread of this tale. So you must tell it yourself. How often I have read of your love. Since I am now but a fairytale, so you recite the tale yourself.[27]

Another important love story was adopted by Rūmī from 'Aṭṭār's *Muṣībat-nāma*.[28] It relates to a king who rebuked Majnūn, 'With all the beautiful women in the world, what are all these tales of your passion for one of our local girls? Why have you raised such a ruckus over a simple girl like Laylā?' Rūmī retells the story as follows:

> Those witless idiots to Majnun said of Laylā:
> 'In fact, she doesn't have all that much beauty.
> There're many girls who vie with her in loveliness,
> All just like moons, and in this town they're numerous.'
> 'The form of women', Majnun said, 'is just a cup.
> God gives me wine to drink through her face and shape.
> From Laylā's shape, God gives you vinegar to taste,
> Lest Love lay hand on you and give your ear a twist.' [29]

The vast number of other tales, which have all been adopted from 'Aṭṭār's *mathnawī*s by Rūmī, unfortunately make too long a list to discuss or even mention here.[30] Aside from Rūmī's creative borrowing of tales and legends from 'Aṭṭār, which demonstrates the close relationship between the two poets, Rūmī also paid careful attention to the respective contexts and contents of 'Aṭṭār's stories. The similarities between the two poets are actually so great that one could almost say that Rūmī had 'Aṭṭār's mystical *mathnawī*s and teachings directly before his eyes or indirectly present in his mind when composing his grand Sufi epic.[31]

Let us briefly consider the impact of ʿAṭṭār's *Conference of the Birds* on Rūmī's *Mathnawī*. If Rūmī did not literally recount the story of the journey of the birds and their trials and tribulations passing through the seven cities of love, one can nonetheless observe the influence and impact of ʿAṭṭār's *Manṭiq al-ṭayr* 'between the lines' of the *Mathnawī*. Not only 'between the lines': there are many instances in the *Mathnawī* where Rūmī alludes directly to ʿAṭṭār's avian epic.[32] In fact, it may be said that Rūmī followed quite directly in the footsteps of ʿAṭṭār, making his own way through the seven valleys of love, enumerating the stages one by one. In certain verses Rūmī more or less hints at the vicissitudes that are experienced when traversing the various valleys, utilizing his own individual lexicon and vision, but disregarding ʿAṭṭār's formal narrative structure.

Let us just look at Rūmī's vision of one—the first—of these valleys, that of Spiritual Quest (*ṭalab*). In the following verses, gleaned from various books in the *Mathnawī*, he offers his own view and original approach to this valley:

The quest itself is the best
Pathfinder of the quest.
Take both your hands:
Apply them to the quest.[33]

*

Discomforts of the quest
Will guide a seeker at last
to find his lover's quarter.
So through pain and grief
Mary found her relief
At the palm-tree's base.[34]

*

O Lord, you are the source,
the genesis of this quest in us,

Just as freedom from injustice is
    but a kind of grace of your justice.[35]

*

Your dry lips issue you this communiqué:
'This fitful fever leads to *aqua vitae*.' ...
This quest is like the rooster's singing at dawn
And thus declaring the arrival of morning.[36]

Each of 'Aṭṭār's other valleys, such as 'self-sufficiency' (*istighnā'*), 'Divine Unity' (*tawḥīd*), 'bewilderment' (*ḥayrat*), and 'annihilation' (*fanā'*), Rūmī also describes after his own fashion, although he discards the formal narrative framework of 'Aṭṭār's allegory. In the history of Persian Sufi poetry perhaps the most celebrated verse ever written about Love is the following line describing the 'Valley of Love' in the *Manṭiq al-ṭayr*:

Reason is smoke but Love's like fire in this valley:
When Love comes in, reason at once flees away.
In Love's hot passion and melancholic frenzy
Reason is a master without authority:
Love's work is not made to measure
Of reason born of mother nature.[37]

Rūmī directly paraphrases these verses of 'Aṭṭār in the following verses from the *Mathnawī*:

Reason's just a sentinel, but let the Sultan walk by there,
And watch miserable reason crawl beneath the stair.[38]

*

When it comes to exegesis of *Eros*
Reason is as good as an ass
That slips in mud. In exegesis
    Of lovers' rules and on Love's rite
    Eros alone discourses right.[39]

Rūmī's monumental collection of lyric poetry, the *Dīwān-i Shams-i Tabrīzī*, is also heavy-laden with the musky fragrance of 'Aṭṭār's inspiration and redolent with resonances of the earlier poet's symbolism, style, similes, imagery and poetic devices. Many of Rūmī's lyrics were consciously composed as exercises in appreciative imitation (*istiqbāl*) of 'Aṭṭār's ghazals. To the educated reader it is obvious that Rūmī often had certain verses of 'Aṭṭār in mind when composing his own lyrics. For example, in one of 'Aṭṭār's ghazals, in which the word *'ishq* ('love') is repeated as a rhyme at the end of each verse, the identical pattern of metre and rhythm pattern is utilized in a ghazal by Rūmī on the same theme. The initial two verses of 'Aṭṭār's ghazal read:

'aql kujā pay barad shīva-yi sawdā-yi 'ishq
bāz nayābī bi-'aql sirr-i mu'ammā-yi 'ishq
'Aql-i tū chūn qaṭra'īst mānda zi daryā judā
chand kunad qaṭra'ī fahm zi daryā-yi 'ishq

How can reason ever get a grip
Upon the wont and wit of Love's passion?
By reason you'll never discover
The *trobar clus* of Love's riddle.
Your reason's like a drop of water
Fallen far away from the ocean.
How much does a drop comprehend
Of Love's vast ocean? [40]

These lines bear comparison with the following ghazal by Rūmī composed in the same meter and rhyme:

Bāz az ān kūh-i Qāf āmad 'anqā-yi 'ishq
bāz bar-āmad zi jān na'ra u hayhā-yi 'ishq
Fitna nishān-i 'aql būd, raft un bi-yiksū nishast
har ṭaraf aknūn bibīn fitna-yi darvā-yi 'ishq

Once again from behind Mount Qāf
The phoenix of love has flown back.

Once again from the spirit's depths
The clamour and cries of love arise.
Uproar and riot were telltale signs
Of Reason, yet these all have fled:
Cast up now everywhere instead
You see the riotous *mêlée* of love.[41]

If we compare the following ghazal by 'Aṭṭār (the first two couplets of which were cited above) with a ghazal composed in the same rhyme scheme and the same meter by Rūmī the extent of the latter's emulation of the former is again evident:

Bū-yi zulfat dar jahān afkanda'ī/ khwīshtan rā bar karān afkanda'ī.
Az nasīm-i zulf-i mushk-afshān-i khwīsh/ ghulghulī andar jahān afkanda'ī.
Vaz kamāl-i nūr-i rū-yi khwīshtan / ***ātashī dar 'aql u jān afkanda'ī.***
Vaz furūgh-i la'l-i rūḥafzā-yi khwīsh/ ***shūrishī dar baḥr u kān afkanda'ī.***
Mīnayā'ī dar miyān-i 'āshiqān /'āshiqān rā dar gumān afkanda'ī.
Bar umīd-i waṣl dar ṣaḥrā-yi dil/ ***bīdilān rā dar fughān afkanda'ī.***
Rū-yi chūn mah zi āsitīn pūshīda'ī/ khūn-i mā bar āsitān afkanda'ī.

The fragrance of your heavy tress
Has filled the world with loveliness.
Alas! You set yourself all at once
Aside and then vacate your place.
The fragrance of your musky hair
Whose scent the breeze bears everywhere
Has thrown up out a delirious gurgle
Beneath the restless ocean of the world.
With fire in the soul your perfect face glows:
You stoke it first, then fan the bellows
And brilliance in the mind ignite.
The gleam of your ruby lips painted bright
With furious passions fill the sea and land.
Although among lovers you're not found,
You tantalize your lovers with suspense,
You leave them to tremble in the balance—

Your lovers then, bereft of heart, are left
To tread the barren plains of the heart.
It's you who rouse in them anguished sobs
Of grief yet leave them still to cherish hopes
Of meeting you. Then you withdraw, eclipse
Yourself, conceal your moonlike countenance
From them and thus our blood you spill
Carelessly as we loiter on your doorsill.[42]

The above seven verses merit comparison (as far as can be seen through the dusky veil of translation) with the following six verses by Rūmī that parallel ʿAṭṭār's (*mathnawī ramal*) metre and rhyme scheme exactly. There are a number of particular instances (vv. 30818b, 30819b, and 30825b, highlighted in bold italics in the texts of both poems) where Rūmī uses three hemistiches from ʿAṭṭār's ghazal, including them (*taḍmīn*), in fact literally duplicating them in his own poem.

(30816) *Bū-yi mushkī dar jahān afkanda'ī*
mushk rā dar lā-makān afkanda'ī.
(30817) *Ṣad hazārān ghulghul z'īn bū-yi mushk*
dar zamīn u āsimān afkanda'ī.
(30818) *Az shu'ā'-i nūr u nār- khwīshtan*
ātashī dar ʿaql u jān afkanda'ī.
(30819) *Az kamāl- laʿl-i jān-afzā'yi khwīsh*
shūrishī dar baḥr u kān afkanda'ī.
(30820) *Tū nahādī qā'ida-yi ʿāshiq-kushī*
dar dil-i ʿāshiq kishān afkanda'ī.
(30825) *Pur-dilān rār hamchū dil bishkasta'ī*
bīdilān rā dar fughān afkanda'ī.

You've released in the world a musk-like fragrance
So the void is scented with that musky incense
And a manifold ripple of musk seems to seethe—
Its aroma then, cast aloft throughout heaven and earth.
All this brilliance in the soul and the mind you ignite
From the shine and the gleam of your fire and light.

From your lips, just like rubies painted radiant bright,
You've unleashed such furious passions that fill all the lands
And the seas. It was you who established the ethos
Of the slaying of lovers, who set in their hearts
Amour's pull and the sway of all matters erotic.
All those stout-in-heart you break just like hearts;
Those bereft of their heart, you've abandoned to sighs and to sobs. [43]

As can be seen from selected verses of the two ghazals cited here, both in regard to formal metrical similarities and stylistic metaphorical resemblances as well as in respect to theosophical topoi, terminology and mystical content, Rūmī's direct appropriation of 'Aṭṭār's imagery for his own uses is evident. The number of ghazals written by Rūmī, in which he relies and follows upon 'Aṭṭār's inspiration, is by no means small but interests of space preclude any further such comparisons.

However, setting aside the stylistic and aesthetic similarities between the two poets, there are fundamental differences regarding both their poetic sensibilities and their philosophic articulation of the Sufi tradition. Firstly, the lyric poetry of Rūmī everywhere exhibits greater maturity and variety of both theme and content, as well as more passion, rapture, ecstasy, and mystical intoxication than the verse of 'Aṭṭār. Secondly, most of 'Aṭṭār's ghazals are devoted to the theme of the beloved's absence and the lover's separation from him/her, whereas Rūmī's lyrics are overwhelmingly consecrated to celebrating the lover's consummation and realization of divine union, having been inspired by ecstatic states of rapture, intoxication and intimacy with the beloved. For this reason, since in Rūmī's lyrics the burning pangs of separation are much less often expressed,[44] so much more joy and delight can be intimated from his ghazals than from 'Aṭṭār's. And that of course, is one of the secrets underlying Rūmī's greater popularity and fame. Yet, despite Rūmī's obvious pre-eminence in the Persian Sufi poetic tradition, both as a poet and a mystic, 'Aṭṭār's words have their own individual savour and unique style of expression. His ghazals in particular, both in sense—content, and in themes—topoi, with their extravagant, excessive quality of boasting and audacity, are inimitable and unrivalled in their mastery of the Persian Sufi poetic tradition.[45]

II. ʿAṬṬĀRIAN FRAGRANCES IN SHABISTARĪ'S *GARDEN OF MYSTERY*

Shaykh Maḥmūd Shabistarī (d. after 740/1340) was another important Persian poet deeply influenced by ʿAṭṭār.[46]

A Sufi poet who belonged to the generation immediately following Rūmī and preceding Ḥāfiẓ, he was the author of one of the most remarkable and original compositions in the entire history of Persian literature, *Garden of Mystery* (*Gulshan-i rāz*), a poem notable for its brevity (it is only one thousand lines long) and conciseness of expression combined with extraordinary depth of theological and theosophical insight. It was composed in the same metre as ʿAṭṭār's *Book of Divinity* (*Ilāhī-nāma*, that is, the *mathnawī* metre of the *baḥr-i hazāj*). In the exordium to this work, Shabistarī acknowledges, with utter humility and devastating honesty, ʿAṭṭār's achievement as the true measure of poetic genius, describing his own lowly rank in the canon of Persian Sufi poetry in the following verses:

> Of my own verse and rhyme I have no shame.
> There is but one ʿAṭṭār each millennium.
> Could the mysteries of a myriad universes
> By such an idiom and mode of expression
> Be put to verse, it's still but scraps and detritus
> from the store of ʿAṭṭār.
> My verse is made by hazard, not by design;
> I'm not a demon who's tapped an angel's line.[47]

Here the poet explicitly acknowledges his own work to stand on the shoulders of the sage of Nishapur. Shabistarī admits that his own poetry conveys at best a whiff of the musky fragrance of ʿAṭṭār's inspiration, but this fragrance is purveyed to the reader not by mimesis of the earlier poet in homage to his memory but in travesty to his inspiration, but rather presented to us by having been infused in the poet through *tawarrud*, that is, by the spontaneous, simultaneous inspiration of a single theme and image into the hearts of two poets sharing like sensibilities. In short, he annnounces that he shares common theosophical ground with ʿAṭṭār.

The profound impact of ʿAṭṭār's symbolic terminology and metaphysical imagery upon Shabistarī's poem is obvious to anyone acquainted with both their work. Here, interests of space preclude offering any more than a few of the more salient examples to demonstrate this influence. Take, for instance, the following verse from ʿAṭṭār's *Manṭiq al-ṭayr*:

ʿArsh-i ʿālam juz ṭilismī bīsh nīst/ ū'st u bas, īn jumla ismī bīsh nīst

This universe and the divine Throne
Is all just one magic talisman:
He alone exists: and all the rest
Are mere names which mean naught.[48]

This merits comparison with the theology and imagery of the following two verses in Shabistarī's *Garden of Mystery*, in which the later poet gives the gist of ʿAṭṭār's verse in similar doctrinal terms and with parallel imagery, comparing the Eternal Being with temporal existence:

Qadīm u muḥdath az ham judā nīst/ ki az hastī-st baqī dā'imān nīst
Hama ān'ast va-īn mānand-i ʿAnqā'st/ juz az Ḥaqq jumla ism bī musammā'st

Eternity a parte ante and living beings are not
Two separate things apart,
For nothingness itself in animate Existence
Forever and ceaselessly exists.
Existence is all there is:
All else but God is phoenix-like
—Phenomena without Noumena.[49]

Both in terms of metaphysical imagery, mystical theology, Sufi terminology and poetic imagery, the respective verses are quite similar, suggesting the probable influence of 'Aṭṭār on Shabistarī's expression.

'Aṭṭār's famous *qaṣīda* on *tawḥīd* (a poem carefully imitated, both in metre and meaning, by later Sufi poets including Rūmī and Maghribī) contains the following verse describing the various modalities of divine manifestation and theophany in the world.

Īnjā ḥulūl kufr buvad, ittiḥād ham/ k'īn waḥdatī-st līk bi-tikrār āmada

Incarnation here is infidelity;
Unification too is blasphemy.
All is one Unity, whose emanation
Proceeds by way of repetition.[50]

Segments of the wording of this verse and the totality of 'Aṭṭār's meaning were later directly adopted, imitated and then rephrased by Shabistarī in this verse:

Ḥulūl u itiḥād īnjā maḥāl-ast/ ki dar waḥdat du'ī 'ayn-i zalāl-ast

Incarnation is here all impossible
And unification inconceivable.
Duality within such Unity
Is utter error, total fallacy.[51]

Yet, the more telling examples of 'Aṭṭārian fragrances wafting through the *Garden of Mystery* appear in the final quarter of the poem where the most sublime flights of Shabistarī's poetic genius are found. In fact, surveying the whole spectrum of Islamic mystical poetry, these three-hundred-odd lines (vv. 714ff.) represent the pinnacle of all symbolic poetry in the Persian Sufi tradition. In this final section, Shabistarī rends aside the veil of Sufi symbolic discourse with a directness and clarity unrivalled by any previous writer and unmatched by any subsequent Persian poet. Whereas his precursors in the tradition, such as 'Aṭṭār, Rūmī, Sa'dī and Niẓāmī, tried to draw a veil over the more abstruse aspects of the Sufi symbolic lexicon and conceal their esoteric terms and truths in hermetic hints couched in cryptic and paradoxical imagery, Shabistarī devotes all his exquisite poetic diction here to rendering an exposé of the lexicon of Sufi mystical terms.

These include the 'Cupbearer' (*Sāqī*), the 'Theophanic witness' (*shāhid*), the 'Christian child' (*tarsābacha*), the 'idol' (*but*), the 'cincture' (*zunnār*), 'Christianity' (*tarsā'ī*), and the 'Tavern of Ruin' (*kharābāt*).

The most significant of these terms, in respect to erotic theology at least, is the 'Christian child' (*tarsābacha*). Exegetes both of a secular-fundamentalist and religious-formalist bent who are unable to penetrate behind the veil of mysteries are always disturbed and confounded by this symbol when it appears in Persian literature. They are especially bemused by its apparition in Ḥāfiẓ's—supposedly 'non-mystical'—poetry (see below). Nonetheless, the 'Christian child' is one of the most important symbols in 'Aṭṭār's poetry,[52] as can be seen, for instance, in the following ghazal which is consecrated to this symbol (two verses of which are cited here):

All at once my heart and soul
Have become the prey of the Christian child.
I've been shorn of all my glory
And made the shame of all the world
By passion for her tresses' tip.
But anyone who finds a token of her
Suspires, loses heart—
Such is the way and the wont
Of that Christian child, of course,
Which is why I am her lunatic. [53]

This same disturbing Christian girl, who had led Shaykh Ṣan'ān blessedly astray from his conventional, formalistic faith, enrapturing him by her beauty and initiating him into the higher idolatry of the religion of love, also reappears in this ghazal by 'Aṭṭār:

That gypsy Christian girl, of folly so full—
Idol of the soul—walked from her convent drunk,
Her bell and wine held in palm, and her hand
Laid upon her girdle, with holy icon held to her heart,
Deploring us Muslims, she hawked her wine.
'For sale! I've wine!' She sang, as if ashamed.
But when on her tress and her lips and her eyes
I gazed, all at once on the throne of my heart
That sovereign moon took up seat, such that she
Became my heart-lord and suzerain. I fell down,
Her bounden slave, thrown down before those bright feet.[54]

Shabistarī echoes these verses by 'Aṭṭār when he describes the spiritual ideal and symbolic meaning of this same 'Christian child' in the lexicon of Sufi symbolism as follows:

The Christian child, that 'idol'
Is but a symbol of light that's pure and manifest
From the faces of idols: iconic forms of her theophany.
All hearts she welds together, conjunct:
Sometimes, the lutanist, she sweeps the strings;
Sometimes, the Saki, she purveys the wine.

Shabistarī's description is heightened and further elaborated in its succeeding lines:

What a bard—whose key of grace
Chimes such measure, it sets aflame the coffers
Of a hundred pietists, a myriad pharisees...!
And what a Saki—whose beaker's brew
Bereaves of self and stirs to ecstasy
Two hundred men of over seventy.
Drunken in a stupor, if she comes at dusk
To the *khānaqāh*, she shows the Sufi's piety
To be but cant—all spells and conjury.

If at dawn, for matins she goes into a Mosque,
No man therein she leaves in sober sense, of self cognizant.[55]

We may also see from the following verses how that same 'Christian child', who had roused such passion and anxiety in 'Aṭṭār as a theophany of the divine Beauty, had also visited Shabistarī, rendering him so intoxicated with her beauty that he cast off all his pretence of faith and tossed away all his love of infidelity down at her feet, as the following verses by Shabistarī (following those just cited) so eloquently describe:

Like a drunk in masquerade, she goes in the Madrasa
—The judges and the jurists there, she leaves in dire straits.
Not just the judges does she befuddle,
The puritans, from love of her are shorn
Of kith and kin, of house and home.
One man from her becomes an 'infidel',
Another—pure and 'faithful'.
It's she who fills the world with such mêlée and misery,
From her come all these woes and ills.
The Tavern of Ruin blooms
With life and health from her lips;
Her visage beams light and lustre
Upon the mosque. Thus, everything
For me by her seems now easy:
Because I see through her the possibility of liberty
From this egocentric heresy: my soul-of-infidelity.[56]

The esoteric symbol of the 'Christian child', who appears as a 'Vintner', 'Barmaid', 'Cupbearer' or 'Bartender' hawking wine to Muslims—a kind of archetypal *puer aeternus* within the Persian poetic imagination personifying the epiphany of God to the heart of the spiritual aspirant—makes its apparition time and time again in Persian Sufi poetry from the time of Sanā'ī down to early modern times. So let us now finally turn to look at some verses by Ḥāfiẓ directly inspired by 'Aṭṭār's tale of Shaykh Ṣan'ān, where perhaps a glimpse of this epiphanic figure and a whiff of this Christian maiden's wine may be caught.

III. Scent of a Woman: 'Aṭṭār's Christian Maiden in Ḥāfiẓ's *Dīvān*

Her perfumed tray of roses,
The casket of her tiny lips
So redolent with ambergris—
For me her sensual fragrance is but one
Whiff of that sweet grace
Which is the lovely odour sent
Me by my own 'Aṭṭār's scent.

—Ḥāfiẓ[57]

Although generally recognized as Persia's most eminent lyric poet (*shā'ir-i ghanā'ī*), Ḥāfiẓ (d. 792/1389) is also the supreme master of what might be called the 'erotic theosophical lyric' (*ghazal-i 'āshiqāna-yi 'ārifāna*). Even more intensely and more deeply than either Rūmī or Shabistarī, he had succumbed to 'Aṭṭār's dynamic spirituality, had imbibed his melancholic romantic passion, was steeped in his inspired consciousness and had been swept off his feet by the wildly unconventional temperament of the mystical non-conformist or *qalandar* who appears as the supreme Sufi adept throughout all of 'Aṭṭār's works. One could even say that in the entire *Dīvān* of Ḥāfiẓ hardly a single ghazal can be found in which the spiritual presence and passionate fervour of 'Aṭṭār cannot be vividly felt.

'Aṭṭār's spiritual presence makes a visible epiphany in Ḥāfiẓ's verse by means of several apparitions of the same 'Christian child' symbol which we witnessed above in the verse of Shabistarī. The child dons a number of different disguises in the *Dīvān* of Ḥāfiẓ, appearing for instance as a Christian boy (*tarsābacha*) in this verse:

A Christian boy who admired wine anyway
Spoke beautifully. He said, 'Toast the man
Or woman in whose face we can see purity and joy.[58]

In the first three lines of Ḥāfiẓ's most famous erotic ghazal, which a number of commentators of a secular orientation insist on interpreting as descriptive of merely human, temporal love, rather than spiritual, divine love, this same Christian child appears as a flirtatious wine-selling maiden with her blouse ripped open, drunk with a cup of wine in hand, seating herself by the poet's bedside one midnight, in these verses:

> Her hair was still tangled, her mouth still drunk
> And laughing, her shoulders sweaty, the blouse
> Torn open, singing love songs, her wine cup full.
>
> Her eyes were looking for a drunken brawl, her lips
> Ready for jibes. She sat down
> Last night at midnight on my bed.
>
> She put her lips close to my ear and said
> In a whisper these words: 'What is this?
> Aren't you my old lover—Are you asleep?' [59]

In another of Ḥāfiẓ's verses, this Christian child appears again, his or her lips uttering the same 'taunts' and 'jibes' described in the second stanza above:

> A young wine-seller's boy stepped tauntingly
> From the door; 'Wanderer, wake up!'
> He said, 'The way you walk has the stain of sleep.'[60]

In his mystical commentary on the *Dīvān* of Ḥāfiẓ, written in the early 17th century, Sayf al-Dīn 'Abū'l-Ḥasan 'Abd al-Raḥmān Khatamī Lāhūrī gives an interesting interpretation of the first verse of the former ghazal (22), explaining it and the entire poem according to the Sufi (and Platonic) doctrine of the ascending hierarchical degrees of love, from form, matter and humanity, up to the transformal, immaterial and the divine, as follows:

> Shaykh Ādharī (may God bless his soul) in his *Jewels of the Mysteries* (*Jawāhir al-asrār*) states that, 'The ecstatic sayings of the masters are the product of the experience of the luminous unveilment or theophanies pertaining to sensory forms (*tajallī-yi ṣūrī*). This sort of sensory theophany occurs in all phenomenal forms, but its experience varies according to the different ontological levels of the various loci of theophany. Thus, for Moses, it was manifest through the burning bush; for Imām Ja'far Ṣādiq, it was experienced in the form of the spoken word; for Shaykh Ṣan'ān it manifested in the form of a young Christian maiden (*tarsābacha*); for lovers it is experienced through the phenomenal forms of their sweetheart, which likewise should be considered as a theophany pertaining to sensory forms, as is obvious from the tales of (the great pairs of lovers such as) Majnūn and Laylā, Khusraw and Shīrīn, Warqa and Gulshāh, Vīs and Rāmīn, and all the other celebrated pairs. The initiated adept of Shīrāz composed this peerless ghazal after this same style, as if to say: "That Transcendent Loved One was luminously unveiled to me in the form of a sweetheart with dishevelled curls, blushing, lips laughing and drunk"'.[61]

Mystics of the Persian Sufi tradition, as Lāhūrī's commentary reveals, clearly understood the path of Sufi symbolism to wend its way (albeit with a number of interesting erotic bends and twists) straight from the alleyway of Shaykh Ṣan'ān's beloved *tarsābacha* girl, whose immortal romance was narrated in 'Aṭṭār's the *Manṭiq al-ṭayr*, more or less directly down to her theophany in a ghazal as a drunken maiden at the bedside of Ḥāfiẓ. So it is hardly odd that by far the clearest instance of the apparition of the archetypal symbol of this Christian child in Ḥāfiẓ's Dīvān actually relates to 'Aṭṭār's story of Shaykh Ṣan'ān and the Christian maiden.[62]

If we set aside the high romances of Yusūf and Zulaykhā, Farhād and Shīrīn, and the tragic desert affair of Laylā and Majnūn, this story remains no doubt one of the most popular romances in Persian Sufism.[63] In what remains the most deeply passionate tale of love in all his *mathnawīs*, 'Aṭṭār relates how that same theophany of Divine Beauty—she who is both the 'Idol' and the 'Christian child'—managed to suddenly seduce and convert a respected and venerable spiritual master into a wildly unconventional Sufi who contemplated divine Beauty through her female form. Prior to his fateful encounter with this *femme fatale*, he had been known for his pious and ascetic nature, as ʿAṭṭār relates:

> For fifty years this shaykh
> Kept Mecca's holy place, and for his sake
> Four hundred pupils entered learning's way.
> He mortified his body night and day,
> Knew theory, practice, mysteries of great age,
> And fifty times had made the Pilgrimage.[64]

As the story goes, the master, who lived in Mecca near the Kaʿba, one night dreamed that he was prostrating before an idol in a city in Byzantine Anatolia. He interpreted his dream to be a divine portent of a trial that God had sent him. Accordingly, he set out for Anatolia with a group of some one hundred of his most loyal followers. Arriving in a certain town, he saw a lovely Christian girl, symbol of the divine Beauty, standing unveiled on a balcony. Not only did he at once lose his heart to her, but she ravished his exoteric Muslim faith away from him as well. The pious master became a devotee of the higher idolatry of the religion of love, a convert to her 'true infidelity' (*kufr-i ḥaqīqī*), a change of heart celebrated in these verses by Maḥmūd Shabistarī:

> Be free of shame and name—hypocrisy and notoriety—
> Cast off the dervish cloak, tie on the cincture
> And like our master, be inimitable in 'infidelity'
> If man you be: unto a Man commit your heart entirely.
> Give up your heart to the Christian child;
> Free yourself of all denial and affirmation.[65]

This spiritual doctrine of conversion from 'illusory Islam' (*islām-i majāzī*) to 'real infidelity' (*kufr-i ḥaqīqī*) in the Sufi literature enunciated here, did not of course originate with ʿAṭṭār's allegory of Shaykh Ṣan'ān, and can be traced back at least to Ḥallāj (d. 922).[66] It is worth mentioning in this context that Shabistarī's exhortation here to become a man 'like our master' constitutes a direct allusion to 'Aṭṭār's tale of Shaykh Ṣan'ān, and refers to the verses in which the Shaykh actually casts off his dervish cloak and binds himself ('ties on the Christian cincture: *zunnār*) in fidelity to a Christian girl, who appears in the tale as a symbol of the theophany of divine Beauty.[67] Lest one wonder at the change of gender—a 'man' in Shabistarī's *Garden of Mystery* switches to a 'maid' in 'Aṭṭār's *Conference of the Birds*—it may be recalled that the metaphysical reality of 'man', and, by extension, the 'lover' and 'beloved' described by both poets transcends the female-male dichotomy. Did not 'Aṭṭār himself claim of Rābī'a in the *Manṭiq al-ṭayr*, that 'she was not a maid but rather a myriad men' and exhort his reader to 'become a *man* like Rābi'a'?[68]

It should be noted that in 'Aṭṭār's account the story of Shaykh Ṣan'ān is recounted by the hoopoe, leader and guide of the troupe of birds, in order to spur them onwards in the mystical quest towards the fabulous Sīmurgh, King of all the birds. As the hoopoe tells the questing fowls in 'Aṭṭār's account, the only provisions wayfarers may take with them on this quest are love and pain:

> Love thrives on inextinguishable pain,
> Which tears the soul, then knits the thread again.
> A mote of love exceeds all bounds; it gives
> The vital essence to whatever lives.
> ...Islam and blasphemy have both been passed
> By those who set out on love's path at last;
> Love will direct you to Dame Poverty,
> And she will show the way to Blasphemy.
> When neither Blasphemy nor Faith remain,
> The body and the Self have both been slain;
> Then the fierce fortitude the Way will ask
> Is yours, and you are worthy of our task.[69]

Now this very story is retold and reshaped, both by cryptic hint and direct reference, in line after line of Ḥāfiẓ's *Dīvān*. Ḥāfiẓ explicitly encourages the mystic to follow Shaykh Ṣan'ān's ethics of detachment step by step and emulate his erotic theology. The sweet fragrance of this wonderful romance, replete with refined points of ethics and profound wisdom, continuously wafts through the garden of Ḥāfiẓ's lyricism. In the following verse, which is also the sole instance in his *Dīvān* where Ḥāfiẓ alludes directly to the story of Shaykh Ṣan'ān, he sums up the central moral of 'Aṭṭār's mystical romance, delivering the same homily found in Shabistarī's last-cited verses, to abandon all fear and shame of losing one's fair name:

If you profess yourself a devotee of
The highway of most noble Love
Never give a second thought for name
Or what men say will be 'ill-fame',
Recall the cap and gown
Of great Shaykh Ṣan'ān—
For months in hock, put in
The wine-seller's shop for pawn.[70]

Aside from this one verse, there are literally thousands of other instances in the *Dīvān* of Ḥāfiẓ where the poet clearly alludes to symbols, tales, ideas or the interpretation of ideas from one or another of 'Aṭṭār's works, and versifies these in his own inimitable and illuminating way. Consider, for example, the following verse:

Pardon me, please, if my rosary
Bead's string has snapped.
But my hand lay touching the forearm
Of a cupbearer with silver legs.[71]

Anyone familiar with 'Aṭṭār's *Manṭiq al-ṭayr* cannot fail to notice that this line harbours another direct reference to the romance of Shaykh Ṣan'ān and his Christian sweetheart. Just like the aged Sufi shaykh, Ḥāfiẓ portrays himself in this verse as head over heels in love with the Christian girl, throwing himself down prostrate before her feet, so that his verse paraphrases the following scenario in the *Conference of the Birds* in which Shaykh Ṣan'ān's disciples formed a circle around him, offering him their counsel and admonition:

'My sheikh', urged one, 'forget this evil sight;
Rise, cleanse yourself according to our rite.'
'In blood[72] I cleanse myself', the sheikh replied;
'In blood, a hundred times, my life is dyed.'
Another asked: 'Where is your rosary?'
He said: 'I fling the beads away from me;
The Christian's belt is my sole sanctuary!'
One urged him to repent; he said: 'I do,
Of all I was, all that belonged thereto.'[73]

The following verse by Ḥāfiẓ also patently functions as a verse-parallel (*naẓīra*) of exactly the same speech (in the second couplet just cited above) uttered by Shaykh Ṣan'ān in 'Aṭṭār's *Manṭiq al-ṭayr*:

I've made ablutions with my tears
For people of the Path always
Say this: 'First purify yourself—
Then gaze upon the one who's pure.'[74]

The following verse from Ḥāfiẓ's *Dīvān* also constitutes the Shiraz poet's creative reinterpretation of the same speech from 'Aṭṭār's *Manṭiq al-ṭayr*:

In Sufi gowns
    And rosary beads
        No drunken joy
            Is ever found.
It is from publicans
    That strength of heart
        To quest for this delight
            Solely must be sought.[75]

These three verses from different ghazals by Ḥāfiẓ are also inspired by the same section cited above from the tale of Shaykh Ṣan'ān:

As I was praying, suddenly
    Within my mind appeared your eyebrow's curve
A state overcame me;
    The prayer-niche was filled with cries.[76]

*

I fear I'll lose all faith
    For your eyebrow's prayer-niche
Robs all mental
    Presence from my praying heart.[77]

*

Only one who absolves himself in the bitter blood
    Of the heart, may perform
Ritual prayers within the crescent-niche
    Of her eyebrows.[78]

To be exact, their probable source of inspiration is the following couplet penned by 'Aṭṭār, where a pedantically religious follower of Shaykh Ṣan'ān bids him foreswear his erotic passion and stick instead to the safe path of ritual prayer:

One counselled prayer; he said: 'Where is her face
That I may pray towards that blessed place?'[79]

But setting this famous romance aside, innumerable other verses in Ḥāfiẓ's *Dīvān* are heavily scented with the fragrance of 'Aṭṭārian inspiration. For example, the opening line of 'Aṭṭār's famous ghazal

Biyā ki qibla-yi mā gūsha-yi kharābāt-ast
biyār bāda ki 'āshiq ni mard-i ṭāmāt-ast.

Come along! For the way we face
    in prayer is towards the tavern corner.
Pass round the wine, for no man's a lover
    who's caught up in idle chatter.[80]

—constitutes the obvious source of inspiration for this verse of Ḥāfiẓ:

Maqām-i aṣlī-yi mā gūsha-yi kharābāt-ast
khudā-yash khayr dahad har-ki īn 'imārat kard

Before all time, our primordial
Degree was in the tavern corner:
God grace with goodness he
Who raised high this edifice.[81]

Moreover, 'Aṭṭār's reference in the above verse to 'idle chatter' (*ṭāmāt*)—a key Sufi term referring to bombastic, grandiose, often senseless utterances made by Sufis in states of rapture—and his assertion that no man is a lover who engages in such bombastic talk and chatter, is certainly directly replicated by Ḥāfiẓ in this verse:

Mā mard-i zuhd u tawba u ṭāmāt nīstīm
mā-rā bi jām bāda-yi ṣāfī khiṭāb kun

Men we are not of
Ascetic strife,
Of pious contrition,
Or bombastic speech
Discourse alone to us
Of cups of wine
Strained pure and fine.[82]

The pluralistic religious vision of Ḥāfiẓ's Persian Sufism, which is expressed in the following famous verse:

Whether we are drunken or sober, each of us is making
For the street of the Friend. The temple, the synagogue,
The church and the mosque are all houses of love. [83]

—both in respect to imagery and Sufi doctrine is certainly squarely based upon the following verse from 'Aṭṭār's *Dīvān*:

> Each of us is making for the street of the Friend and yet
> Where's the humble man, drunk in spirit, manifest? [84]

Many other such parallels between 'Aṭṭār and Ḥāfiẓ, both in respect to poetic imagery and mystical doctrine, might also be adduced here, yet any attempt to trace and track all the various sorts of Nishapurian fragrances wafting through the rosebeds of Shīrāz, to record and relate verse by verse the sweetness of 'Aṭṭār's lyrical genius in the ghazals of Ḥāfiẓ would itself become a task as prolonged as the proverbial tresses of the beloved, of which Shabistarī complained,

> Long are the tales of the Beloved's tress.
> What can be said?
> It's a place of profoundest mysteries.[85]

And in recounting the sweet twists and snarls of which, 'Aṭṭār found himself bemused,

> In her musky tresses so many kinks and snarls can be found,
> It would take one hundred hands to count each strand. [86]

And over those curls' exegesis, Ḥāfiẓ too confessed himself bewildered and at wits end:

> The commentary upon the twists and kinks
> Of the Beloved's curls can never be abridged,
> —This tale itself is too strung out.[87]

But since we cannot guzzle down the sea, of necessity we must limit ourselves to a cupful of water: 'if I cut short my tale—may your life be long'—as the adage goes.

One point is worth reiterating in conclusion. No Sufi ever quotes the saying of another Sufi unless his purpose be to illustrate his own inner contemplative experience and describe his own mystical states. No doubt, Sufis often have and do still relate one another's words verbatim, but their intent through such citation is always to represent their own interior revelations and personal spiritual experiences. At the same time, the Sufi sages' and poets' independent outlook in respect to expression of their contemplative visions and spiritual experiences does not at all preclude copious cultural borrowing from one another. In the diffusion of the scent and the sweetness of Sufi spirituality and in the raising high the standard of mystical poetry, few poets in Persian literary history played such a central role as did 'Aṭṭār. Indeed, in the firmament of Persian Sufi poetry his verse still remains 'the star of every wandering bark' which sails upon the ocean of the Spirit, even if he himself, who knew this truth all too well, confessed himself in these spheres to be but a lost and errant wanderer:

> A myriad stars of guidance to the mysteries
> Rove through the heavens of 'Aṭṭar's verse
> And yet his lot is like this vagrant
> Firmament, to wander itinerant and headless. [88]

NOTES

1. Translation of the poetry is by Leonard Lewisohn who also acknowledges his gratitude to Terry Graham's and Christopher Shackle's editorial assisance.

2. Rumī, *Kulliyāt-i Shams yā Dīvān-i Kabīr*, ed. B. Furūzānfar (Tehran, 1355 Sh./1976), vol. 2, p. 22, ghazal 563, v. v. 5961.

3. Citing this famous verse in his *Sharḥ-i aḥwal wa naqd-u taḥlil-i āthār-i Shaykh Farīd al-Dīn Muḥammad 'Aṭṭār-i Nayshābūrī* (2nd ed., Tehran, 1374 Sh./1995), pp. 72, Badī' al-Zamān Furūzānfar comments that 'it cannot be found in any of the ten ancient mss. which formed the basis of my edition of the *Kulliyāt-i Shams*; and is only present in a single ms., that published in Lucknow, and in some later manuscripts.'– Tr.

4. *Dīwān-i Ḥāfiẓ*, ed. Parvīz Nātil Khānlarī (Tehran, 1362 Sh./1983), p. 494, ghazal 239: 1. All references to Ḥāfiẓ below are to Khanlarī's edition.– Tr.

5. *Manṭiq al-ṭayr*. Ed. Sādiq Gawharīn. Tehran: 'Ilmī u farhangī 1374 A.Hsh/1995, 10th

reprint (Hereafter MT), pp. 246-247 (vv. 4456-4457). It should be noted in this context that the two words used, 'passion' (*shūr*) and 'lovers' (*'ushshāq*), have a meaning besides the literal sense. In the terminology of Persian music, shūr designates a musical mode (*dastgāh*), and *'ushshāq* denotes a certain melody in that mode.

6. *Dīwān-i 'Aṭṭār*. Ed. Taqī Tafaḍḍulī. Tehran: Bungāh-i Tarjuma wa Nashr-i Kitāb 1345 A.Hsh/1967 (Hereafter Dt), p. 604, ghazal 757: 1.

7. Dt, p. 606, ghazal 760: 1-2.

8. Rūmī, *Mathnawī*, ed. Nicholson, vol. 2, p. 267.

9. *Dīwān-i Ḥāfiẓ*, p. 794, ghazal 389. This verse, which is excised from Khānlarī's edition, occurs in variant readings found in two of his earliest Mss.– Tr.

10. Amīr Sayyid 'Alī Hamadhānī, *Mashārib al-adhwāq: Sharḥ-i Qaṣīda-yi Khamriyya Ibn Fāriḍ Miṣrī dar biyān-i sharāb-i maḥabbat*, ed. M. Khwājawī (Tehran, 1362 Sh./1983), p. 64.

11. Ṣamad Muwaḥḥid, ed., *Majmū'a-i āthār-i Shaykh Maḥmūd Shabistarī*, (Tehran, 1365 Sh./1986), p. 69.

12. One of the best examples of such narrative leaps can be found in the wonderful tale of Ṣadr-i Jahān in the third book (vv. 3686ff.) of the *Mathnawī*. In the middle of his account, Rūmī abruptly abandons the theme and starts another story relating to—the apparently extraneous subject of—the apparition of the Angel Gabriel to Mary, mother of Jesus, where he presents us with one of the most beautiful and eloquent accounts of the apparition of an angel to a human being in all of world literature. Then, he suddenly recalls the lover of Ṣadr-i Jahān who has been left standing stranded on the road to Bukhārā waiting for his tale to be told. So the poet says, 'Let's abandon the candle of Mary while it is still burning—for that wild, impassioned lover is on his way to Bukhārā.' In Western literature one can perhaps find such poetic flights in the novels of Victor Hugo, in Tolstoy's *War and Peace*, perhaps—but amongst Rūmī's forebears in Persian literature, such as Sanā'ī, Niẓāmī and 'Aṭṭār, one rarely finds similar lyrical flights and poetic leaps from the frame-tale into another, often higher, narrative sphere.

13. MT, p. 12, v. 22.

14. MT, p. 200, v. 3583.

15. MT, p. 200, v. 3587.

16. MT, p. 14, vv. 251-252.

17. Dt, p. 212, ghazal 270, v. 9.

18. *Mathnawī*, vol. 1, vv. 1607, 1609.

19. Although this particular verse is absent from Furūzānfar's edition of Rūmī's *Dīvān-i Kabīr*, it has been traditionally ascribed to Rūmī; see, e.g., Nūrānī Viṣāl's

introduction to his edition of *Muṣībat-nāma* (Tehran, 1354 Sh./1975), p. vii.– Tr.

20. I have not been able to locate this story in any of 'Aṭṭār's *mathnawīs*.– Tr.

21. Furūzānfar, *Mākhadh-i qaṣaṣ wa tamthīlāt-i Mathnawī* (Tehran, 1362 Sh./1983), pp. 80-81, traces the source of this story back to the *Maqālāt-i Shams*. – Tr.

22. *Muṣībat-nāma*, pp. 340-341.

23. For the Old Harpist's tale, see *Mathnawī*, vol. 1: 1913-1950; 2104-2112; 2161-2222; also cf. Furūzānfar, *Mākhadh-i qaṣaṣ... Mathnawī*, pp. 20ff. – Tr.

24. *Muṣībat-nāma*, p. 297; Furūzānfar, *Mākhadh-i qaṣaṣ... Mathnawī*, pp. 193-194.

25. *Muṣībat-nāma*, pp. 139-140; Furūzānfar, *Mākhadh-i qaṣaṣ...Mathnawī*, pp. 173-17.

26. *Mathnawī*, vol. 5, 1891.

27. *Mathnawī*, vol. 5, 1896-1897.

28. *Muṣībat-nāma*, pp. 279-280; Furūzānfar, *Mākhadh-i qaṣaṣ... Mathnawī*, pp. 8-9.

29. *Mathnawī*, vol. 5, 3286-3289.

30. To give a few examples of celebrated Sufi stories adopted by Rūmī from 'Aṭṭār's various *mathnawīs*: There is the story of the bird-catcher who had caught a bird who begged, 'Don't kill me! If you set me free, I'll give you two or three pieces of advice.' Then there is the tale of Azrael, the angel of death, who gazed angrily at a man, causing him to take refuge in Solomon, begging him to whisk him off to India. Finally, there is the anecdote of the fool who became the companion of Jesus, calling for the latter to bring a collection of bones to life for him.

31. This is especially evident in Rūmī's treatment of Satan or Iblīs, which is in many respects almost identical to 'Aṭṭār's approach to the same subject.

32. Cf. *Mathnawī* (vol. 2, 3758): 'The discourse of the princely birds of Khāqānī is mere empty sound. What has become of the discourse of the birds of Solomon?' (*Manṭiq al-ṭayr-i sulaymānī kujā'st?*).

33. *Mathnawī*, vol. 3, 979.

34. *Mathnawī*, vol. 2, 98. The verse contains an allusion to the Koranic account (19:23) of Mary's pains during childbirth.

35. *Mathnawī*, vol. 1, 1337.

36. *Mathnawī*, vol. 3, 1441, 1444.

37. MT, p. 187, vv. 3346-3347.

38. *Mathnawī*, vol. 4, 2110.

39. *Mathnawī*, vol. 1, 115.

40. Dt, p. 368, ghazal 448, 1-2.153.– Tr.

41. Rumī, *Kulliyāt-i Shams*, ed. Furūzānfar, vol. 3, pp. 133-134, ghazal 1311, vv. 13876, 13881.

42. Dt, p. 606, ghazal 760 (skipping six lines).

43. Rūmī, *Kulliyāt-i Shams*, vol. 6, p. 173, ghazal 2900.– Tr.

44. This is exactly the same observation attributed to Rūmī by his biographer Shams al-Dīn Aflakī; see *The Feats of the Knowers of God (Manāqeb al-'arefīn)*, tr. John O'Kane (Leiden, 2002), vol. 3, 131, pp. 152-153. – Tr.

45. It should also be mentioned that Rūmī paid close attention to 'Aṭṭār's *Mukhtār-nāma*, especially in regard to its themes and that he drew heavily from this selection in his own quatrains.

46. For further discussion of 'Aṭṭār's influence on Shabistarī, see Ṣamad Muwaḥḥid, ed., *Majmū'a-i āthār-i Shaykh Maḥmūd Shabistarī* (Tehran, 1365 Sh./1986), introduction, p. 11; 'Abd al-Ḥusayn Zarrīnkūb, 'Sayrī dar Gulshan-i rāz', in his *Naqshī bar āb* (Tehran, 1368 Sh./1989), pp. 256-294.– Tr.

47. *Gulshan-i rāz*, in *Majmū'a-i āthār-i... Shabistarī*, vv. 56-57. See also Leonard Lewisohn's edition of the same work: *Gulshan-i rāz (Bāgh-i dil)*, ed. H. Ilāhī-Qumsha'ī (Tehran, 1377 Sh./1998), p. 41, vv. 85-86.

48. MT, p. 8, v. 127.

49. *Gulshan-i rāz*, in *Majmū'a-i āthār-i... Shabistarī*, p. 96, vv. 702-703.

50. Dt, p. 817.

51. *Gulshan-i rāz*, in *Majmū'a-i āthār-i... Shabistarī*, p. 85, v. 449.

52. See Leonard Lewisohn's essay in *Attar and the Persian Sufi Tradition* (© IIS and IB Tauris, 2006), pp.241-255.

53. Dt, p. 158, ghazal 210.

54. Dt, no. 822, pp. 659-660.

55. *Gulshan-i rāz*, in *Majmū'a-i āthār*, vv. 969-974.

56. *Gulshan-i rāz*, in *Majmū'a-i āthār*, vv. 975-979.

57. *Dīwān-i Ḥāfiẓ*, ghazal 52, v. 6.

58. *Dīwān-i Ḥāfiẓ*, ghazal 119, v. 8. Tr. Robert Bly and Leonard Lewisohn.

59. *Dīwān-i Ḥāfiẓ*, ghazal 22, vv. 1-3. Tr. Bly and Lewisohn.

60. *Dīwān-i Ḥāfiẓ*, ghazal 414, v. .2. Tr. Bly and Lewisohn.

61. *Sharḥ-i 'irfānī ghazalhā-yi Ḥāfiẓ*, ed. Bahā' al-Dīn Khurramshāhī et al. (Tehran, 1373 Sh./ 1994), I, p. 426.

62. For further discussion of the influence of 'Aṭṭār on Ḥāfiẓ, see Bahā' al-Dīn Khurramshāhī, *Ḥāfiẓ-nāma, Sharḥ-i alfāẓ, i'lām, mafāhīm-i kilīdī va abyāt-i dushvār-i Ḥāfiẓ*, (Tehran, 1372 Sh./1993), vol. 1, pp. 52-53; and for the specific impact of the Shaykh Ṣan'ān tale on Ḥāfiẓ, see ibid., vol. 1, pp. 183-184; 385-387.– Tr.

63. See C. Shackle's essay in *Attar and the Persian Sufi Tradition* (© IIS and IB Tauris, 2006), pp. 165-197.– Tr.

64. MT, vv. 1186-1188; tr. Dick Davis and Afkham Darbandi, *The Conference of the Birds* (Middlesex, 1984), p. 57.

65. *Gulshan-i rāz,* in *Majmū'a-i āthār,* p. 103, vv. 966-968.

66. For a study of this doctrine, see Leonard Lewisohn, *Beyond Faith and Infidelity: The Sufi Teachings and Poetry of Maḥmūd Shabistarī* (Richmond, 1995), ch. 8.

67. MT, vv. 1385-1387. The shaykh's love is by no means simply a sensual infatuation with her mortal beauty, since the girl is described by 'Aṭṭār as having been endowed with 'a spiritual nature; in the Path of Jesus, who is *Spiritus Dei,* she was possessed of myriad sorts of wisdom' (v. 1208).

68. MT, vv. 580-583.

69. MT, vv. 1174-1175; 1178-1181. Tr. Davis and Darbandi, *Conference,* p. 57.

70. *Dīwān-i Ḥāfiẓ,* ghazal 79, v. 6.

71. *Dīwān-i Ḥāfiẓ,* ghazal 202, v. 8

72. The original Persian reads *khūn-i jigar,* literally meaning 'the liver's blood', but by extension signifies bitterly wept tears that are 'bloody tears torn from the heart', or 'tears of blood drawn out of the gut'.

73. MT, vv. 1269-1274. Tr. Davis and Darbandi, *Conference,* p. 61.

74. *Dīwān-i Ḥāfiẓ,* ghazal 258, v. 7.

75. *Dīwān-i Ḥāfiẓ,* ghazal 390, v. 4.

76. *Dīwān-i Ḥāfiẓ,* ghazal 69, v. 1.

77. *Dīwān-i Ḥāfiẓ,* ghazal 392, v. 7.

78. *Dīwān-i Ḥāfiẓ,* ghazal 127, v. 4.

79. MT, v. 1275. Tr. Davis and Darbandi, *Conference,* p. 61.

80. Dt, ghazal 46, p. 33.

81. *Dīwān-i Ḥāfiẓ,* ghazal 127, v. 3.

82. *Dīwān-i Ḥāfiẓ,* ghazal 388, v. 5.

83. *Dīwān-i Ḥāfiẓ,* ghazal 78, v. 3. Tr. Bly and Lewisohn.

84. Dt, ghazal 30, v. 4. Thus, one may compare Ḥāfiẓ's first hemistich *Hama kas ṭālib-i yārand, chi hushyār chi mast...,* with 'Aṭṭār's first hemistich: *Hama kas ṭālib-i yārand u līk...*

85. *Gulshan-i rāz,* in *Majmū'a-i āthār,* p. 98, v. 760.

86. Dt, ghazal 226, v. 2. *Attar and the Persian Sufi Tradition* p.172.

87. *Dīwān-i Ḥāfiẓ,* ghazal 41:5.

88. Dt, *Qaṣīda* 26, p. 820.

'Allegory of Worldly and Otherworldly Drunkenness', folio from the *Divan* of Ḥāfiẓ, by Sultan Muhammad *ca.* 1531-33

The Principles of the Religion of Love in Classical Persian Poetry

It's a matter of creed for me: goblets of wine,
My love's lips just like rubies, this is my doctrine
I won't forsake. Puritans, I offer you apologies. —Ḥāfiẓ[1]

The Genealogy of the Religion of Love in Persian Poetry

From ancient times Persian literature has featured many references to the 'Religion of Love' (*dīn-i 'ishq or madhhab-i 'ishq*), represented as being the only true faith, the creed most acceptable in the eyes of God. In classical Persian poetry, the most famous verses where this concept seems to have first been vocalized are by Rūdākī Samarqandī (d. 329/940):

What use is it to serve one's turn to face
The Mihrab in your prayers, when all your heart
Is set upon the idols of Taraz and of Bukhara?
What God accepts from you are love's transports,
But prayers said by rote He won't admit.[2]

Rūdākī's younger contemporary, the Sufi martyr Manṣūr al-Ḥallāj (d. 304/922), when asked which religious creed he followed, in the same vein pronounced: 'I follow the religion of my Lord' (*Anā 'alā madhhabī rabbī*).[3] Ḥallāj's bold claim was embraced by many of the later Sufis, such as his follower 'Ayn al-Quḍāt Hamadhānī (executed 526/1132) who alluded directly to the 'Religion of Love' in this key passage in his *Tamhīdāt*:

> The lovers follow the religion and the community of God. They do not follow the religion and creed of Shāfiʿī or Abū Ḥanīfa or anyone else. They follow the Religion of Love and the Religion of God (*madhhab-i ʿishq wa madhhab-i khudā*). When they behold God, this visionary encounter of God (*liqā-yi khudā*) becomes their religion and creed; when they see Muḥammad, this visionary encounter with Muḥammad (*liqā-yi Muḥammad*) becomes their faith (*īmān*). When they behold Iblis, that station's vision becomes to them [the meaning of] infidelity. Thus it is possible to understand what the faith and religion of this group consists in, and from whence derives their 'infidelity'.[4]

Underlining the scriptural basis for their radical theology of love, Sufis referred to the famous Koranic verse (V:54), affirming that God, notwithstanding recusants among mankind, will bring forth a people 'whom He loves and who love Him' (*yuhibbuhum wa yuhibbunahu*). They interpreted this verse as referring to the saintly company who are lovers of God and who in turn are beloved by God. Similarly, one finds another Koranic verse (II:165) that states: 'The believers are stauncher in their love of God.'

The earliest major Persian Sufi poet to make love an axiom of an individual mystical theology and personal religious creed was Sanāʾī of Ghazna (d. 525/1131). In one verse, Sanāʾī thus identifies both his Sufi path (*ṭarīqat*) and his sectarian creed (*kīsh*) as being 'Love' itself:

> Why do you ask about my creed and faith tradition?
> It's clear. My creed is *Eros. Amor* is my canon.[5]

Similarly, in another verse, Sanāʾī incites the reader to 'Rise up and show forth the high stature of Love, for the Muezzin has said: "Rise up to pray!"'[6] Here, the poet informs us, like Rūdakī before him, that true ritual prayer in practice is enacted by a lover and in reality sustained by love. 'The divine Muezzin,' he declares, 'summons you to rise up and demonstrate in every action of your life the high stature of love, since life itself is nothing but one constant *adoratio amoris*.' The same teaching, using a similar metaphor we find enunciated a few generations later by Jalāl al-Dīn Rūmī (d. 1273):

In *eros* lies transcendent heights which rise
And summon us to music that's immortal
Save to seek those erotic highs
One should never dance, never revel.[7]

Niẓāmī of Ganja (d. 598/1202), the leading author of epic romantic poetry in Persian literature, must also be counted among the chief prophets of the Religion of Love in Persian *belles lettres*. In his romantic epic poem *Khusraw and Shīrīn*, Niẓāmī teaches that the only role that man is fit to play in the entire theatre of Existence is that of the lover in the following verses, where Love is featured as a kind of *Anima Mundi*:

Naught else but love's my labour: that's my logo;
So long as I'm alive, don't offer me another motto.
All face towards love to supplicate in every
Temple under Heaven's eye. The galaxy
Itself wouldn't have an earth unless across
The surface Eros' water coursed to save its face.
Become a slave to love! All righteous thought consists
Of this, for that's the task of the heart's adepts.
The cosmos *is* love in sum and all the rest deceit;
Save *Amor*'s play, all else's an idle game and sport.[8]

Niẓāmī, long before Newton, had posited that the entire scale of creation and nature was permeated by a reciprocally acting gravitational force that he named 'Love':

Attraction works on human temperament its lure
And that attraction sages predicate of love,
So when you ponder this in depth then you'll perceive
That *Eros* holds the cosmos up: all stands through love,
And if once *Eros* lose its grip on Heaven's wheel
The great globe itself would forfeit its bloom and weal.[9]

Niẓāmī continues to glorify love in the next verses and describes the fundamental message of his poetic composition as a summons to Love:

> Devoid of *Eros*, life appeared to me soulless.
> I sold my heart and in its place a soul purchased.
> I've filled the rims and cornices of the globe
> With *Amor*'s smoke. I've made the eyes of reason doze.[10]

After Niẓāmī, the next great prophet of the Religion of Love in Persian poetry was 'Aṭṭār of Nishapur (d. 618/1221 or 627/1229). Like the poets mentioned above, in line with the Koranic doctrine of love (v:54), 'Aṭṭār believed the only commendable and worthwhile connection between man and God to be a Lover-Beloved relationship. Like many other Muslim mystics before him, 'Aṭṭār emphasized that the superiority and pre-eminence of Adam over the other angels lay in Adam's/man's love-passion and agony.[11] In fact, in 'Aṭṭār's spiritual teachings, the cure for all psychological and spiritual ailments lies in the transformative suffering and passion of love (*dard*).[12] That is why he asks for that passion to be increased:

> Give me an ounce of pain, O you
> Who cure all pain, for left without
> Your pain, my soul will die.
> To heretics let heresy apply,
> And to the faithful—grant them faith;
> But for the heart of 'Aṭṭār, let
> One ounce of your pain remain.[13]

Muḥyī al-Dīn ibn al-'Arabī (d. 638/1240) of Andalusia in Spain, known as the *Shaykh al-akbar*, the 'Supreme Shaykh', was one of the first Sufis to describe the Religion of Love in a specifically ecumenical sense. In his theosophical works composed in Arabic he gave explicit theological expression to a separate religious creed that he called the Religion of Love (*Dīn al-ḥubb*)—a faith which embraced all manifestations of reality while encompassing yet transcending their divergent appearances. The following verses are among the most famous and admired lines ever composed in Islamic—if not world—civilization on the theme of this transcendental erotic religious creed:

Pasture between breastbones
And innards.
Marvel,
A garden among flames!

My heart can take on
Any form:
For gazelles, a meadow
A cloister for monks,

For the idols, sacred ground,
Ka'ba for the circling pilgrim,
The tables of the Toráh,
The scrolls of the Koran.

I profess the religion of love;
Wherever its caravan turns
Along the way, that is the belief,
The faith I keep.[14]

The other great Arab mystical poet—a contemporary of Ibn 'Arabī who lived in Egypt—who belonged to this same School of Love was 'Umar ibn Fāriḍ (d. 633/1235). Ibn Fāriḍ's entire poetical oeuvre is one immense paean in praise of love's mysteries, a hymn composed in expositions of the subtleties, sublime degrees and mystical states of Islamic erotic spirituality. Although all his verse was composed in Arabic, many of the later literati of Persia honoured his genius by giving him the honorary title of 'Ḥāfiẓ of the West.' In his famous Wine Ode (*Qaṣīda-yi khamriyya*), Ibn Fāriḍ describes in great detail the quickening qualities and effects of wine upon the spirit—wine being used here as an allegory for the elixir of love and its intoxication.

To relish the spirit and convey the taste of this wine and also to give a small glimmer of the grandeur of the sublime station of love in his verse, it must suffice here to cite the two opening and two concluding verses of this poem:

In memory of the beloved
  We drank a wine;
    We were drunk with it
  Before the creation of the vine.

The full moon its glass, the wine
  A sun circled by a crescent;
    When it is mixed
  How many stars appear.

Its two final verses are:

For there is no life in this world
  For one who lives here sober;
    Who does not die drunk on it,
  Prudence has passed him by.

So let him weep for himself,
  One who wasted his life
    Never having won a share
  Or measure of this wine.[15]

Over the rest of this period of what might be called 'the Golden Age of Classical Persian Literature'—the thirteenth through fifteenth centuries—the 'Religion of Love' (*madhhab-i 'ishq*) became increasingly celebrated in verse by major poets such as Jalāl al-Dīn Rūmī (d. 672/1273), Saʿdī (d. c.691/1292) and Ḥāfiẓ. Their contributions to this central current of Islamic erotic spirituality are discussed below.

The Religion of Love in Rūmī

It will be worthwhile to explore Rūmī's own understanding of this transcendental *madhhab-i 'ishq*, since he devotes so many verses of his ecstatic poetry to claiming that the religion of love transcends not only Islam, but every other religion as well. He thus begins one long ghazal announcing the supra-Islamic nature of Eros as follows:

In the summa of *Amor*
    Where's the idiom of Islam?
Where's one master exegete
    Of *Eros* whose lore suffices
    To crack the code of its complexities?[16]

In another ghazal, he delineates the above distinction between the esoteric creed of love and exoteric Islam in greater detail:

Get lost! The lover's *secta amoris* is the reverse
Of other faiths and creeds, for from the one you love
Untruth and perfidy beats kindness and sincerity,
Her fabrications inspirations, her sin all gratuity,
All ill from her is just, her taunts all right and meet,
Her temple is the Ka'ba, soft as silk her adamant.
The nettle's sting from her I think is better than
Rose petals and sweet basil. If scoffers then poke fun
And say: 'It's deviant—this crooked creed you've got!'
Reply: 'Her eyebrow is my creed. I bid for it
And laid down life for this—the 'creed of crookedness'!
It's all I need, I'll waste no words. Go read the rest in silence.' [17]

We find him again extolling in a quatrain the superiority of love's 'crooked creed' over the so-called 'straight' way of formalistic Islam:

Her tresses' tip our fetish-cult
    And eye that's drunk and impudent—
That is the creed which we adopt.

They say that healthy piety is something else,
Assert sound faith is different, aside from these,
But from their 'sound faith' and 'creed of wholesomeness,'
We choose her deviant, uneven ways and crookedness. [18]

This same strict distinction and difference between the formal creed of Islam and the higher transcendental religion of love is reaffirmed by Rūmī in a number of other quatrains in his *Dīvān* as well. In the following two quatrains, he maintains that love's esoteric faith supersedes conventional religion and is something apart from the other world's traditional sects:

Erotomaniacs is what we are: lovesots;
The Muslims they're a different lot. We're spindly ants;
King Solomon's another sort. A burning, aching heart
And sallow faces seek of us: the abattoir's on a different street. [19]

*

Know it for certain that the lover's not a Muslim
For in the creed of love there's neither infidelity
Or faith; since once you fall in love, you have no body,
No soul, no heart, no mind: who ain't like this, ain't nothin. [20]

In his mystical epic 'The Rhyming Spiritual Couplets' (*Mathnawī-yi ma'nawī*), Rūmī frequently celebrates the 'Religion of Love' as well. The following verse from his *Mathnawī* constitutes his most famous statement concerning the pre-eminence of this higher *secta amoris*:

Love's state is apart
From religions and faith
God is the lover's creed—
God is the lover's state.[21]

The Religion of Love in Ḥāfiẓ

Ḥāfiẓ is Persia's greatest erotic lyricist who remains the supreme—and in some senses the last—prophet of the Religion of Love in Persian literature. There are many verses in his ghazals that appear as a manifesto of this transcendental creed:

Both human beings and spirits take their sustenance
From the existence of love. The practice of devotion
Is a good way to arrive at happiness in both worlds.[22]

*

Become a lover; if you don't, one day the affairs of the world
Will come to an end, and you'll never have had even
One glimpse of the purpose of the workings of space and time.[23]

In Persian literature, the prophet Ḥāfiẓ's collected poems (*Dīvān*) constitute a sacred scripture which, just like the works of Sa'dī, is a faithful reflection of the divine Beloved's countenance. Both poets were prophets; both composed poetic scriptures that remain miracles of beauty in Persian, their verses appearing as divine signs (*āyat*) of loveliness and grace. For Ḥāfiẓ, the entire world reflects the grace and loveliness of the divine countenance, for, insofar as 'Wheresoever you turn, there is the Face of God' (Koran, II:115), that Face reveals and casts a ray of the infinite divine beauty in the mirrors of man, cosmos, microcosm and macrocosm:[24]

Your beautiful face divulged to us
The chapter and verse of divine grace,
Which is why nothing exists
Save grace and comeliness
In our scriptural exegesis.[25]

This same theophany of beauty also cast its ray upon Ḥāfiẓ's verse, gleams of which were reflected through various poetic images such as 'Idol' (*but*), 'Christian child' (*tarsā-bachchih*), 'Magian child (*mugh-bachchih*), 'Cupbearer' (*sāqī*), and 'Friend' (*yār*). When these images are apprehended by any reader attuned to Ḥāfiẓ's symbolic universe, they arouse intoxication and selflessness, freeing one from conceit, self-centredness and egotism. Thus, in the following verse in his *Dīvān*, we see how the 'Magian child' appears to rob the poet of his egocentric faith and initiate him into love's esoteric creed:

> Just when the Magi's child strolled along
>   (The thief of hearts and wrecker of belief)
> At once the Muslim puritan was carried off,
>   From all his friends divorced himself. [26]

Ḥāfiẓ's religion of love teaches devotion to that essential Beauty whose loveliness reappears time and time again in the guise of various symbols among other Sufi poets.[27] This is particularly evident in the lines from the following ghazal, which is one of the most famous erotic poems in all of Persian literature:

> Her hair was still tangled, her mouth drunk
> And laughing, her shoulders sweaty, the blouse
> Torn open, singing love songs, her hand holding a wine cup.
>
> Her eyes were looking for a drunken brawl, her mouth
> Full of jibes. And this being sat down
> Last night at midnight on my bed.
>
> She put her lips close to my ear and said
> In a mournful whisper these words: 'What is this?
> Aren't you my old lover—Are you asleep?'
>
> The friend of wisdom who receives
> This wine that steals sleep is a traitor to love
> If he doesn't worship that same wine.[28]

As the last stanza indicates, Ḥāfiẓ professes that anyone who does not revel in drinking the wine of love to be a heretic and traitor to love's creed (*kāfar-i 'ishq*). This statement makes better sense if we decode the reference to wine as being metaphorical of the theophany of beauty in the raiment of mortal beings. In the most important mystical commentary on the *Dīvān* of Ḥāfiẓ written by Sayf al-Dīn 'Abū'l-Ḥasan 'Abd al-Raḥmān Khatamī Lāhūrī (fl. 17th century in India), the commentator, when explaining this poem, alludes to the particular meaning given to the term 'infidel' or 'traitor' or 'heretic' (*kāfar*) in the philosophy of Ibn 'Arabī, as being 'someone who conceals the existence of God through manifestation of existing phenomena.'[29] Lāhūrī explains that the mystic versed in Sufi erotic theology should not allow phenomena to veil his vision of Noumena, and should realize that the transcendent beauty must—and can only—be contemplated through the translucent veil of human beauty. Paraphrasing Ḥāfiẓ, Lāhūrī states:

> That Transcendent Beloved Being then spoke, stating that any gnostic who is a confidant of the arcane mysteries, who recognizes the true face of such an affair, when given such a wine—that is, beauty and loveliness decked out in the garb of the veiled presentment of a figurative mortal sweetheart—will only end up veiling and concealing this display of God, this divine theophany, unless he becomes a worshipper of beauty (*ḥusn-parast*). This is because it is through the forms of mortal beauty (*suwar-i husniyya*) that God-as-Absolute in reality attracts the hearts of lovers to Himself.[30]

For Ḥāfiẓ, as for the other followers of the religion of love, this adoration of beauty (*jamāl-parastī*) reveals itself through the cult's opposition to the self-aggrandizing *Sharī'a*-oriented Islam of the common Muslim. To relish the taste of this erotic faith, say the Sufi poets, one must divorce old barren reason from the bed (along with its religion pursued for selfish worldly ends) and take the daughter of the vine to spouse instead, just as Iran's greatest bacchanalian poet 'Umar Khayyām (d. c.519/1125–527/1132) taught.[31] Edward Fitzgerald in his classic translation of Khayyām, while slightly misrepresenting the letter, perfectly conveys the spirit of this idea in this quatrain:

You know, my Friends, how long since in my House
For a new Marriage I did make Carouse:
Divorced old barren reason from my Bed,
And took the Daughter of the Vine to Spouse.[32]

Ḥāfiẓ also uses exactly the same terminology to refer to his conversion to this transcendental non-conformist religion of love. He sprinkles his verse with a variety of terms to this end: 'Love's creed' (*madhhab-i 'ishq*),[33] the 'Magian master's faith' (*madhhab-i pīr-i mughān*),[34] the 'creed of inspired libertines' (*madhhab-i rindān*),[35] the 'faith of the Sufi Path' (*madhhab-i ahl-i ṭarīqat*),[36] and, occasionally, simply 'our creed' (*madhhab-i mā*).[37] Among these terms, each of which have a slightly different connotation in his erotic spirituality, the following verses comprise his key statements:

Don't allow the flirty side-glances of beauties
To teach you injustice. We know that in the religion of love
Each act returns with its own consequences. [38]

*

The only prayer apse
The heart of Ḥāfiẓ has
Is your eyebrow's arch
For in our faith
It's you alone, none else
Commands obeisance. [39]

*

Above homage and obeisance to lunatics
Do not seek for more from us, for our sect's master
Professed all intellectualism to be wickedness.[40]

*

'To wear the dervish robe and then to drink wine,
    That's not a rite of true doctrine.'

I said. 'Indeed,' she said, 'but in the Magian
  Master's rite of faith, that's all holy doctrine.'[41]

*

I followed the path of the mad libertines for years—
Long enough, until I was able, with the decree
Of intelligence, to put my greediness into prison.[42]

*

On the spiritual road, being uncooked and raw
Is a mark of unbelief; it's best to move along the path
Of fortune with nimbleness and springy knees.[43]

While much of the poetry of Rūmī, Sa'dī and Ḥāfiẓ has been penned by way of exposition of the Religion of Love, the abstruse spiritual principles of this faith remain virtually unknown to many students of Islamic thought, whether in the East or in the West. Below I will provide an overview of the basic principles of Islam's erotic theology as depicted by the classical Persian poets, illustrated by examples from the Koran and Persian literature:

The Primordial Disposition of Man and the Religion of Love

According to the Koran man was created with an 'original disposition that God instilled within him' (*fiṭrat Allāh*) and formed with a 'fundamentally immutable God-given nature' (*lā-tabdīl li-khalqi'llāhi*: xxx:30). Basing themselves on this evidence from their holy scripture, Persian poets drove this classical theological doctrine several theosophical notches higher, maintaining that man's nature had been already moulded and framed to develop according to the nature of the divine attributes of Beauty, Truth, and Goodness, and inclined to follow the 'Straight Path of Love and Mercy' (*'ishq, maḥabbat, raḥmat*) long before birth. As human beings, we thus enter the world with faith in the divine innately deposited within the depths of our selves, for, according to the Prophet's renowned saying: 'Every child is born according to his original disposition (*fiṭra*); then his parents make him into a Jew, a Christian, or a Zoroastrian.'[44]

Therefore, in the narrow sectarian sense of the word, no one is 'born' a Muslim[45]—much less a Hindu, Buddhist, Christian, Jew, or Zoroastrian—but rather every person is moulded into becoming a 'believer' subject to the influence of their parents, wider society and cultural environment. At the same time, it should be emphasized that all these faiths, setting aside the excrescences, excesses and superfluities to which each has been heir, is quintessentially moulded according to that same God-given 'original disposition' within humankind. Thus, all the world's religions may be viewed as divergent manifestations of that one primordial faith of man, that is, the religion of his original disposition (*fiṭra*).

Each of these faiths, having its own fair share of opportunistic power-seeking, theological deviance, sanctimonious cant, snobbish bias, hypocritical pretence, unctuous piety, priggish affectation, and bigoted prejudice, along with a host of other vices, has become separated from and spurned its sister, considering its fellow travellers in the realms of Faith as damned—apostates or infidels or heretics destined for Hades and Gehenna. Nonetheless, in every religion one can always find a small number of true adepts, saints and men of God who are its spiritually realized gnostics and poets who are attuned to the Divine. Among this elect company one finds few divergences and disagreements save in respect to terminological expressions and modes of ritual practice pertaining to incidental forms of exoteric dogma, which are irrelevant to the quintessential reality of their faith. The true believers within every religion, as Rūmī puts it, are like rays of a single lamp:

If ten lamps are together in one place
  each one is different from the next in form.
You cannot tell apart the light of each
  when you are looking at them, there is no doubt.[46]

Whatever their exterior denomination, the soul and spirit of the faithful reflects their insight into God's comprehensive Mercy which encompasses and embraces all men, good and ill alike:

> Besides the soul and understanding in
> the ass and cow, there's sense and soul in man
> that's different. Again, besides this human sense
> and intellect, the saintly souls in bliss
> have higher cognizance. The souls of brutes
> possess no unity; in that *anima vitalis*
> don't seek for oneness. If a single base
> man eat some bread, another man who's base
> will not be full, and if one brute bears weights
> his neighbour's not distressed. No, he rejoices
> to hear he's died or dies of jealousy
> when good accrues to him or profit sees
> has come to him. Thus, souls of dogs and wolves
> are set in castes apart: yet there're no halves,
> but only wholes in lions' souls.[47]

Therefore, it is wrong to assert we enter into the world devoid of all faith and belief and only subsequently personally select a religion for ourselves. On the contrary, each person is born with love for the good, beautiful and true innately instilled within him. If he doesn't deviate from the 'straight path of his original disposition', this primordial love will mature and develop within him and direct him along his course in life. The sole purpose underlying the mission of the prophets in the various religions is to bring people back to that original disposition. The reason we need to hearken to their summons is that our original spiritual disposition, exactly like our physical metabolism, is constantly plagued by myriad diseases, afflicted with moral and/or metaphysical amnesia due to various hindrances which impede its healthy progress and block its natural advancement. The different heavenly scriptures of the world's faiths brought by their prophets are analogous to medicinal cures for these ailments. They are reminders to men, while their various legal codes—Canon Law (*sharī'a*)—must be considered as different paths of development and maturation adapted to the diverse religious needs of various peoples. Insofar as the original disposition of man is one and the same, and all the prophets have been sent by the One God, it is unreasonable to assume that the religions of mankind should or can differ in their fundamental principles from each other. The mission of the prophets is thus precisely tailored to suit the original disposition of man, comprising a summons to contemplate the good, beautiful and true. In the words of Maḥmūd Shabistarī (d. after 740/1339)

That Day when Faith was written down
within the heart, the clay of man
was moulded in the human form,
The word of God was sent down then
and holy books revealed to men
so you'd recall your vow again.[48]

In several places in the Koran, allusion is made to the triad of these transcendent qualities that bring delight to the heart and salvation to the soul. As Rūmī puts it:

Since prophethood's the guide to liberty,
Believers get their liberty from prophets free. [49]

In the pursuit of goodness, knowledge and beauty, we receive such a sense of joy and experience so much rapture and delight that we even forget personal sorrow and grief; we become as Sa'dī says, steeped so deep in the delight of contemplation, that 'all the world's woes have no effect.'[50] In Islamic erotic spirituality, this is best illustrated in the famous Sūrah XII (Joseph) in the Koran, where we read how Zulaykhā, the wife of the Pharoah of Egypt, summoned a group of her Egyptian women friends to her palace. She wanted them to see her favourite slave-boy Joseph with whom she was madly infatuated, for themselves. As soon as he strutted in the room, the ladies, who had all previously found fault with Zulaykhā for her passion for him, immediately recanted their prudery, being smitten by the overwhelming loveliness of his 'human form divine'. Wildly besotted with him, they slit their wrists with the same knives she'd given them to peel fruit, exclaiming: 'This is not a human being, but some gracious angel!' (XII:31). By preaching a religion of passionate love (*'ishq*), poets such as Ḥāfiẓ or Sa'dī similarly intend to advocate the idea that by falling in love and observing the courtesies of lover and beloved, men and women may realize transports of consciousness unbeknownst to normative conformist religious piety. In this fashion, we may attain felicity and salvation both in this world and the next, which is, by the way, precisely the sense intended by Ḥāfiẓ's well-known exhortation:

> Go strain your every nerve to gain the high degree of love;
> The benefits will be immense if only you could make this voyage.[51]

Such is also the purport underlying Sa'dī's celebrated description of the mystical 'stages of love' in these verses at the beginning of his *Būstān*:

> If you desire to chart your way across
> This ground, first hamstring all the horses
> You'd use to journey back. Then contemplate
> The mirror of your heart until the state
> Of purity you slowly find. If the perfume
> Of love befuddles you till you're drunken,
> You'll probe about to seek that timeless vow
> You made to God. Your quest's on foot till now,
> But once you're there, you'll fly on wings of love,
> Till certainty the veil of phantasy
> Rends aside and nothing but the Court
> Of Majesty remains to veil your heart.[52]

The Religion of Love and Antinomian Traditions in Islam

A thousand enigmas subtler, finer spun than
A strand of hair lies here, and thus not everyone
Who shaves his scalp can understand the rite of the Wildman.[53]
—Ḥāfiẓ

Like Christianity, Islam harbours many important antinomian traditions. By the eleventh century, antinomian mystics who considered that Islamic ritual practices and the sacred Law (*sharīʿa*) could be dispensed with, leaving them free to commit any transgressions and sins that they wanted to on the basis of their inspired mystical vision and enlightened understanding, had appeared among the Sufis.[54] One of these antinominian traditions that originally developed among early Shiʿite groups was the doctrine of *Ibāḥat* (libertinism).

A variety of terms in classical Persian literature soon became used to refer to these antinomian mystics: *qalandar*s (vagabonds, wild men), *rind* (inspired libertine), *qallāsh* (knave), *mubāḥī* (libertine), *dīvāna* (lunatic) and *lā-ubālī* (daredevil, desperado). The latter term, literally meaning 'I couldn't-care-less,' indicates a cavalier attitude that damns the consequences of all prodigal and immoral conduct. We find many verses by Saʿdī and Ḥāfiẓ praising both the daredevil *lā-ubālī* and the wildman *qalandar* attitude.[55] Saʿdī says:

For learned quartos what use has the reckless lover?
Why should the lunatic's moonstruck mind forbear
To hear the preacher's horatory admonitions?
Why should lovers give a twit about abuse
And calumny from friend or foe? There's not
Much choice in either case: they suffer on the rack
Of love or bear the weight of slurs and smears.[56]

In the following lines, Ḥāfiẓ celebrates the perfect antinomian lover in the person of the Sufi Shaykh Sanʿān who fell in love with a Christian girl, abandoned Islam, and through his apostasy demonstrated his true faith in the Religion of Love:

If you profess yourself a devotee of
The highway of most noble Love
Never give a second thought for name
Or what men say is all 'ill-fame',
Recall the cap and gown
Of great Shaykh Ṣan'ān—
For months in hock, put in
The wine-seller's shop for pawn. [57]

In another verse, Ḥāfiẓ again celebrates the legend of the *qalandar*, referring indirectly to Shaykh San'ān who found faith and piety in binding on a Christian cincture at the bidding of the Christian girl:

What rapturous, enchanting moments
that holy roaming dervish has
who fares through all the stations of
the mystic way, who in the tangled knots
of the Christian girdle that he wears
still tills his rosary and hymns
angelic litanies and prayers.[58]

In these verses, Persia's two most famous love lyricists, Sa'dī and Ḥāfiẓ, boldly announce their avocation of Eros' creed. Making full use of the antinomian vocabulary available in Persian, they declare themselves *Fedeli d'amore* indifferent to the blame and reproach of those cold souls who are disbarred from the throes of erotic passion and thus banned from entry into the precincts of *Amor*. As faithful servants of Love's Path, they understood that 'nothing exists save grace and comeliness'[59] in the pursuit of love and declared themselves ready to succumb to all its passions and temptations.

Although terms such as *lā-ubālī*, *qalandar*, *rind*, *qallāsh*, *mubāḥī*, and *dīvāna* originally had exclusively profane meanings—referring to various types of thugs, hooligans, debauchees, lunatics, profligates, rakes and other ne'er-do-wells of society—they were soon taken over by the Sufis and integrated into the Persian Sufi poetic lexicon, where they were given positive connotations denoting higher degrees of mystical realization. Thus, the profligate became identified with a mystic of high degree, the debauchee with a pious man of prayer, the vagabond equated with a disengaged spirit liberated from sensual desires, the knave a member of the saintliest company, and the lunatic the truly inspired man attuned to the voice of God. Of course, it is easy to see why today many literary critics in secular circles who more often than not utterly are alienated from the traditional symbolic cosmos in which such emblems, symbols, tropes and types all functioned as part of a common 'hermetic' discourse familiar to all connoisseurs of verse, find themselves voicing doubts and disagreements about which sense precisely—profane or sacred, human or divine—such metaphors should convey. Unfortunately, most of the younger generation of Persian-speaking literati, being immersed in secular Western values, no longer recall the higher symbolic connotations of these terms. To their understanding, Ḥāfiẓ thus remains the supreme decadent and hedonist poet, leader of the world's grand debauchees. To complicate matters further, the poetic device of *īhām* (amphibology) allowed the Sufi poets to marry heaven and earth, and, so to speak, condone poetic ambivalence, so that the distinctive allegorical metonymy of terms in the Sufi symbolic lexicon lent a diversification to their usages, allowing them to broadly connote both the colourful, literal 'profane' connotations *as well as* the higher figurative senses pertaining to those transcendental symbolic meanings.

If we approach the transcendental significance of some of these symbols, how the process—and thus the *raison d'être* sustaining—the sublimation of these metaphors occurred is easy to discern. The phrase, 'it is delightful to be mad', for example, poetically speaking conveys a self-evident sense. Understood spiritually, however, the phrase makes no sense whatsoever unless we understand it to imply a madness *above* and *beyond* reason, rather than *below* reason: the lower, irrational—psychotic—insanity.[60] Likewise, the expression, 'the joys of intoxication' makes perfect sense to every secular sensibility attuned to wine's bacchanalian pleasures. But to the philosophical temperament focused on progress in the spiritual life, it makes sense only when it refers to the drunkenness that contemplation of the Beautiful inspires, or as the Sufis say, the ecstatic rapture that the sight of the beauteous visage of the Cupbearer (*sāqī*) arouses in the beholder, stimulating intoxication without any hangover. In the same vein, the joys of freedom extolled by the Sufi poets involve their liberation from the vices of greed, anger, pride, and emancipation from the vanity of ambition for honours and high rank. Liberty is as much a spiritual virtue as license is a moral vice. That wanton witness-of-beauty (*shāhid-i harjā'ī*) celebrated in Sufi mystical poetry is that icon of supreme loveliness, whose ravishingly attractive countenance is everywhere reflected, both in man and nature alike.[61] When Sufi mystics proudly announce that they 'revel in the delights of desire (*havas*),' their apparently sybarite sentiment takes as its transcendental reference point the 'grand desire' of the adept to realize freedom from selfhood, as Rūmī states:

> There lies in no man's head
>   Such desire as lies in mine;
> The desire I sense is such that
>   I'm bereft of all ken of self.[62]

Similarly, Sanā'ī boasts of his own 'desire' (*havas*) animating his poetic inspiration:

> The magic diablerie of conjurers
>   from Indian lands, graces
>   his breath of inspiration;
> The subtle Chinese portraitists,
>   whose art all faces unmasks,
>   lend his desires animation.[63]

In Ḥāfiẓ's verse as well, we find that the fulfilment of desire in love implies a freedom from self-interest and the renunciation of selfish desire:

> My heart—disport
> Your head: loveplay's
> Not jesting business.

Nobody has yet struck
Eros's shuttlecock
With Desire's bat.[64]

Here Ḥāfiẓ contrasts the transcendental nature of 'true love' (*'ishq*) to the pursuit of idle erotic amusement, which in comparison seems but a kind of shallow 'sport' (*bāzī*) and selfish 'desire' (*havas*): this term here having no transcendent mystical implication. In this respect, Ḥāfiẓ often clarifies that the flames of his erotic longing and fire of his desire (*ātash-i havas*) were not inspired by any temporal passion, but that his passion was enkindled in pre-Eternity when the uncreated souls of men first professed divine love for their Lord—

Flushed and scorched in desire's sultry flames today
Ḥāfiẓ's heart not only now aches with woe,
A brand of grief sears him like the anemone
For now, for always—and since pre-eternity.[65]

This type of holy antinomianism and pious libertinism is best described in a ghazal by Rūmī devoted to the 'lovers' and the 'gnostics,' which describes them as a debauched company of profligates and libertines. In this poem he employs all the important technical terms used in Islamic theology to refer to antinomian debauchees, in particular, the *mubāḥī,* a wild libertine who is utterly outside the pale of all Islamic faith and piety, and the *ibāḥatī*: the pursuer of libertine ways. For those who believe that Sufism constitutes a basically heterodox anti-Islamic mystical ideology falsely masquerading under Muslim robes, Rūmī's poem brings unwelcome news, for he immediately subverts his own subversive rhetoric, clarifying that there is a higher mystical significance beneath his profane terms:

Today we've got songs and an amphora
    full of wine and the music of Samā';
A Saki stone-drunk bears us the wine
    among this crowd of wayward libertines.

They're 'far-out' libertines, in fact, they've passed
 beyond existence—not decadent, demented
Dope-fiend types, high on hemp or hash:
 the blacked-out addicts of the lowlife. [66]

In the first line of this ghazal, the 'Saki stone-drunk' (*Sāqī-yi bad-mast*) is a symbol for Rūmī's spiritual master Shams-i Tabrīzī. He also clarifies that this 'crowd of wayward libertines' (*jam'-i mubāḥī*) are lovers, that is, spiritually advanced mystics who have 'passed beyond existence' into a realm where the limitations of the illusory selfhood, with its 'me' and 'thee', are abolished. Such 'libertines' are not lowlife substance abusers giggling time away on hashish, nor common dope addicts huddling among the dregs of society, but transcendentalists who have not only transcended themselves, but have dismissed the Angel of Death from their dominion.[67]

In exactly the same manner as Rūmī, Ḥāfiẓ (supposedly a hedonist and founding father of libertine teachings in Persian poetry) also clarifies that he eschews self-indulgent antinomianism (*mubāḥāt*) in one important verse:

Heart-friend, I guide you well along Salvation's way:
Neither by sin vaunt iniquity nor hawk austerity.[68]

The Sin of Repentance in the Religion of Love

Although Repentance (*tawba*) is normally listed as the first stage of the Sufi path, in the religion of love, repentance came to be considered a reprehensible vice and terrible sin. In a ghazal whose rhyme phrase is 'I have repented' (*tawba kardam*), Rūmī thus quips:

In the sacrament of penitence's sin
 and in the exercise of penance's crime,
Neck-deep I lay, but now of all that sin
 I make amends: my penance was the crime.[69]

In his *Mathnawī* Rūmī describes how the black slave Bilāl, one of the earliest converts to Islam, was tortured by his Jewish owners for his new faith. The Prophet's wealthy companion, Abū Bakr (who eventually emancipated Bilāl) advised him to conceal his beliefs from his cruel overlord. Bilāl, however, was unable to dissimulate and hide his fervour for God, despite being stretched out in the hot Arabian desert sun and beaten with clubs capped with thorns until he bled. In the following verses, we hear Abū Bakr advise Bilāl to 'repent' of his indiscretion, and how Bilāl rejects repentance:

> Again, he said, 'Repent!' Again, at once
> he did, but Eros whisked away repentance.
> Repentance of this ilk he carried on,
> till penance caused him detestation.
> He spoke his faith out loud, his flesh gave up
> to Fortune's frowns, adversity, hardship.
> 'My penitential vows, Oh Prophet, you
> oppose, yet every vein is full of you!
> There is no room in me for *culpa mea*,
> for penance, penitence or penalty!
> All sacraments of penance such as this
> I scorn. Who'd ever spurn eternal bliss?!
> For Eros is a mighty force: I'm trounced
> by his imperious might; I'm crushed;
> In Eros' bitter, vinegary furor
> I'm sweet and luscious—savoury as sugar.'[70]
> ...To be a lover, yet act with patience,
> *sangfroid* to hold to vows of penitence,
> This is, great soul though you indeed may be,
> a senseless, comical absurdity:
> For patience's but a snail, Eros is a dragon;
> the latter all divine, the former only human. [71]

Here we see Love is considered to be a 'sacred sin' that is paradoxically the source of all piety and religious belief. According to this erotic creed, the quintessence of Islam lies in committing the 'divine crime' of love, and to repent of love is sin and heresy. A good flavour of these wildly passionate sentiments that permeate all classical Persian poetry in general and underpin Sufi erotics in particular, can be found in these three verses by respectively Rūmī, Sa'dī and Ḥāfiẓ:

Alas, what sin or crime is this, of which
Repentance of it is but vile wickedness?
Behind, I'd dodge but cannot flee away;
Before, I'd come yet there's no place to stay.[72]

Go tell all men, go let the folk
Be told that I'm a lover and a drunk.
This name and fame, I boast of it,
I'm proud to say all vows I've broke.[73]

The bedrock of our famous repentance seemed
To be tough as granite. Look, the delicate
Glass cup has split the repentance at the first blow.[74]

The most famous illustration of this critical attitude towards the ascetic ideals of 'repentance' in classical Persian poetry is found in 'Aṭṭār's story of the pious Sufi master Shaykh Ṣan'ān, mentioned above. Following the promptings of a dream, Ṣan'ān travelled with a large band of disciples from Mecca to Byzantine. There, seeing an unveiled Christian girl in a window, he was smitten by love. She disdained him at first, forcing him to spend sleepless nights on her doorstep. Eventually, however, she relented and accepted him as her lover, but to test the sincerity of his love, subjected him to several trials—demanding that he renounce Islam, burn the Koran, drink wine, and work for her as a swineherd. He acquiesced to all his beloved's commands, eventually becoming the model pious heretic of the Sufi religion of love. All of Ḥāfiẓ's poetry, as I have shown elsewhere, is saturated by this tale.[75] In the following lines from 'Aṭṭār's account, we hear the Shaykh's disciples urging him to recant and repent of his blasphemous passion. But to all their entreaties, he makes only flippantly sacrilegious replies:

> 'My sheikh,' urged one, 'forget this evil sight;
> Rise, cleanse yourself according to our rite.'
> 'In blood[76] I cleanse myself,' the sheikh replied;
> 'In blood, a hundred times, my life is dyed.'
> ...Another cried: 'Enough of this; you must
> Seek solitude and in repentant dust
> Bow down to God.' I will,' replied the sheikh,
> 'Bow down in dust, but for my idol's sake.'
> And one reproached him: 'Have you no regret
> For Islam and those rites you would forget?'
> He said: 'No man repents past folly more;
> Why is it I was not in love before?[77]

Eventually, the love-spell cast by the girl was broken and the prayers of his distressed disciples, for months at their wits' end on how to win the Shaykh back into fold of Islam, were heard. The swineherd Sufi Shaykh awoke from the dream of Christianity. However, soon after he cut off his Christian cincture and headed back with them to Mecca, she pursued him hotly, tragically dying—a Muslim, of course—in his arms.[78]

Ultimately, the Shaykh did 'repent' of his love passion, but his repentance was not so much a formal 'turning back' as a passage out of exoteric into esoteric Islam—a casting off of the phantasy of conventional faith for the reality of true devotion. Shaykh Ṣan'ān, having passed through the crucible of erotic romantic passion, experienced a fresh conversion to religion based upon the principles of love. He was no longer the desiccated ascetic Sufi of ere but a fiery *Fedeli d'amore*.

The Worship of Wine in the Religion of Love

Classical Persian poems are normally filled with extravagant praise for the cupbearer (*sāqī*), goblet (*sāghar*), wine-vat (*khum*) and drunkenness (*mastī*), winehouse (*maykhāna*), tavern (*kharābāt*), tavern-master (*pīr-i kharābāt*), and so on. Indeed, many of the clichés and stock metaphors in Persian erotic poetry are bacchanalian,[79] with the lover (*'āshiq*) usually described as a witless wanderer (*parīshān*), a headless and footless vagabond (*bī-sar u pā*), a drunkard (*mast*), who is constantly intoxicated (*mast-i mudām*), transported in selfless rapture (*bīkhvīshī*), 'out of his mind' and bereft of self-consciousness (*bīhūshī*). Such bacchanalian terminology is not personally subjective vagaries that express the poet's melancholic moods, but actually cognitively precise descriptions that depict exactly the lover's intoxication during contemplation of the beloved's beauty, his excitement at imagination of her phantom (*khiyāl*) and his rapture at the recollection of her beauty previously witnessed in time-before-time on the Day of the pre-Eternal Covenant (*rūz-i alast*) between man and God.[80]

Since the reflection of the Beloved's beauteous countenance is everywhere cast down and reflected in the 'goblets of phenomena' throughout the Tavern of the Universe, the lover is always intoxicated and bereft of self in a drunken transport. Loving that absolute intellectual Beauty, he attains the spiritual station of 'true idolatry' (*butparastī-yi ḥaqīqī*),[81] which is the inner meaning of Ḥāfiẓ's verse:

> The Friend's reflection cast upon the goblet's surface
> —Her countenance there—in contemplation I've witnessed.
> Of such timeless drunken pleasure, you are, alas, oblivious. [82]

Ḥāfiẓ's 'timeless drunken pleasure' is not of the unessential or accidental kind, but rather substantial, since the intoxication it bestows—unlike the drink made from the vine or imbibed through the heady wine of ambition, pride and thoughtlessness—is not followed by any hangover or morning-after headache. Hence, it can never be nullified by repentance or by the recovery of sobriety. Those drunk on this wine never commit the sin of becoming teetotallers; as Sa'dī says: 'no man drunk on that wine served up at the dawn of pre-Eternity becomes sober until vespers are said on the night of the Day of Resurrection.'[83]

This pre-Eternal 'wine of the Covenant' (*sharāb-i alast*) mentioned so often by Sufi *fedeli d'amore* refers to the recollection of the pledge that was sealed in pre-Eternity (*ahd-i Alast*) between the uncreated souls of Adam and their Lord. 'Am I not your Lord? (*alastu bi-rabbikum*)?' God asked the yet uncreated souls of Adam's offspring. In this unconscious and uncreated state, they professed: 'Yes, we bear witness to it (*balā shahidnā*).'[84] (Koran VII:172) Humankind's troth plighted to God in that atemporal moment of Islam's metahistory comprises the Sufi Religion of Love's unwritten constitution. What is missing from this narration for the ordinary reader is the fact that the word *balā*, which means 'yes' in the above verse in Arabic, signifies 'calamity' as well. The Sufis took the implication of this Arabic linguistic pun very seriously, believing that the human soul in eternity before its incarnation in time had actually committed itself in advance to undergo all life's trials and tribulations.

The 'wine of the Covenant' that the mystic imbibes thus tastes 'bitter' just like the fruit of the vine. Although this wine is quite capable of making a man pass out in a drunken stupor 'under the table', as Ḥāfiẓ says,[85] its 'bitterness' has always been interpreted by the Sufis as an allegory for the pains and troubles man must endure when he mobilizes himself in service to his fellow men. In fact, 'servitude to mankind' is both the best description of love's creed and the best indicator of one's love for God. All questions posed in Love's catechism can be answered with one single riposte: 'Service'.

This 'bitterness' was given an even more creative exegesis by the Persian *fedeli d'amore*, who compared it to relishing the sapiential 'taste' of drunken rapture (*dhawq-i mastī*) in contemplation of the beloved. The pleasure of that vision and their acquiescence to the beloved's will caused its whole bitter taste to turn to sweetness, an experience which Saʿdī's memorable verse celebrates:

For others, the wine of the torments of love
Is gall, but for us, the liquor we imbibe
We take from the hand of the Friend
So it becomes sweet and delicious.[86]

A number of Ḥāfiẓ's verses underscore the same bittersweet sentiment:

> Although the thorn hurts your spirit, the rose asks pardon
> For this wound; the sourness of wine is more easily tolerated
> When one remembers the sweet flavour of drunkenness.[87]

Ḥāfiẓ also boasts of being famed as a drunkard from the very first day of the pre-Eternal Covenant (*rūz-i alast*),[88] and rails against the ascetic who cannot understand that his intoxication with human beauty is a necessary consequence of his vow in pre-Eternity to follow love's religion:

> Oh, ascetics, go away. Stop arguing with those
> Who drink the bitter stuff, because it was precisely
> This gift the divine ones gave us in Pre-Eternity.[89]

Elsewhere, he directs his attention beyond this temporal sphere and speaks of being drunk on the wine of the Covenant:

> How blessed is the man who, like Ḥāfiẓ,
> Has tasted in his heart the wine made before Adam. [90]

That wine is exactly the same whose cupbearer Niẓāmī invokes in his *Sāqī-nāma* within his romantic epic *Sharaf-nāma*:

> Cast sleep away, O Saki, from your eyes
>   and pass to lovers who are pure that wine
> That is purest claret, which all the schools
>   of law accept and sanction as divine.
> Come, Saki, from the village-elder's cask
>   that honey-sweet wine pour into our flask;
> Don't give us wine which legal schools have banned
>   but wine through which Faith's principles are crowned.[91]

Similarly, Ibn Fāriḍ in a key verse from his *Wine Ode* celebrates the 'sin' of his drunken bacchanalian adoration of wine as follows:

But they said: 'You've drunk sin!'
No, indeed, I drank only
That whose abstention
Is sin to me.[92]

THE IMMEDIATE PRESENT MOMENT (*NAQD-I WAQT*) IN THE RELIGION OF LOVE

Since love transforms whatever concerns the past or future into wares consumed in the present and 'now', the devotee of the religion of love lives in the present moment. The lover is always the 'Child of the Moment' (*ibn al-waqt*) as Rūmī put it:

The Sufi is 'a son of the moment';
The word *mañana* is unheard of on the Way.[93]

*

The Sufi is 'a son of the moment';
In quest of purity he holds the moment close
Like a son clings to his father.[94]

In his *Discourses*, Rūmī explains the theosophical doctrine underlying this notion as follows:

Some men look at the beginning, and some men look at the end. These who look at the end are formidable and powerful, for their gaze is fixed on the final issue of things and the world beyond.

Then, there are those who look at the beginning, who are more elect. They say, 'What need is there for us to look at the end? If wheat is sown at the beginning, barley cannot be reaped in the end, or if barley is sown, wheat shall never be harvested.' So their gaze is set on the beginning.

There are others who still more elect: they gaze neither upon the beginning nor do they contemplate the end. Being absorbed in God, neither beginning nor end ever enter their minds.[95]

Since the *fedeli d'amore* who pursue love's creed understand the preciousness of the present moment, they know that time must not be wasted in expectation of any future Resurrection. Anyway, for them the Resurrection shall never come since it has already occurred! That is why Ḥāfiẓ rebukes the ascetic for the emptiness of his promise of a future paradise:

> When Paradise is mine today as cash in hand,
> Why then should I be taken in and count upon
> The puritan's pledge of tomorrow's kingdom? [96]

Sa'dī enunciates this same doctrine in one verse:

> Eternal youth with its great fortune and felicity
> Belongs to he who's next to you; he's never had his day;
> He knows no age: his home's in highest heaven.[97]

Living in the here and now, heaven and earth for the lover becomes transfigured: he becomes a denizen of heaven. 'The Resurrection becomes your very *état d'âme* in the immediate present of Now (*naqd-i ḥāl*)',[98] as Rūmī puts it. Not only is the Resurrection an immediate experience (*naqd-i ḥāl*) for him, but all the great events of history—the myths, legends, and the tales of the heroes and saints of yore—are felt as living experiences apprehended in the present. They are not hoary tales of a bygone past. They represent the ready cash and coinage of the lover's soul, whose shillings and pence he spends here and now. For poets such as Sa'dī and Ḥāfiẓ, the references to the legends of Moses and his revelation on Mt. Sana'i (Koran, VII:142–45), or the tales of Abraham and the tyrant Nimrūd[99] who cast him into the furnace (Koran, XXI:68–69; XXIX:24), are not simply colourful poetic devices—which the Arabic rhetoricians pedantically categorize as being a 'proverbial allusion' (*talmīḥ*)[100]—but actual occurrences within the poet's soul. This interiorization of religious mythology within the psyche of the poet is reflected in Ḥāfiẓ's verse about Moses' vision of God in the Burning Bush:

Here's pitch black night, there lies the Valley of Peace
Before my feet, so where's Moses' light,
Mount Sinai's Burning Bush and the promised sight? [101]

In reference to the story of Abraham being cast into the furnace, likewise Saʿdī says:

Although I'm cast like Abraham into the furnace of
Affliction, it would not matter: glowing with your love
I'd bask among the basil shoots and tulips of your garden.[102]

All the tales of great lovers and the fables of the heroic champions of yore thus become part of the soul's psychohistory. They pertain to the inner journey of the poet. That is why the epic tales of Firdawsī, the versified romances of Niẓāmī, and ʿAṭṭār's story of Shaykh Ṣanʿān's infatuation with the Christian girl comprise the stuff of their verse in the here and now. These are not legends but living facts of the heart that appear constantly in their verse; they are, as Emily Dickinson says, 'Bulletins all day from Immortality'. In a single verse, Saʿdī thus summarizes the entire epic romance of *Khusraw and Shīrīn* by Niẓāmī:

I realized it then, that very first day when
With Shīrīn my affair began: I knew that in
The end, sweet life itself I would abandon.[103]

As Niẓāmī relates, a beautiful Armenian princess named Shīrīn ('Sweet one') was a concubine of the Sasanian monarch Khusraw Parvīz II (reg. 591–628). A stone sculptor called Farhād,[104] renowned for his physical prowess, was a rival of the king for her affections. Recognizing the all-consuming nature of his rival's attachment to his concubine, Khusraw declines to murder him, thinking it more prudent to give his mighty sculptor rival the seemingly impossible task of carving a canal through a mountain to allow for the flow of milk from the pasture to her palace. Even more smugly, Khusraw promises Farhād his concubine as a reward for his efforts should they succeed.

When surprisingly, Farhād meets the challenge and carves out the canal, Khusraw dupes him by telling him that Shīrīn has died, leading Farhād to cast himself off the mountain in despair to his death.

Ḥāfiẓ in a single verse summarizes another romantic legend from Firdawsī's epic *The Book of Kings* (*Shāh-nāma*), as follows:

I have fallen into Patience's lowest pit
Where, empassioned by the candle of Chigil[105]
And, enkindled by love's flame, I have been burnt.
The prince of Turks knows not my good or ill...
    Where's Rustam the champion?[106]

Ḥāfiẓ here compares his condition with that of the Persian hero Bīzhan, son of Gīv and nephew of Rustam.[107] During an adventure in the lands of Turan (Central Asia), Bīzhan encounters Afrāsiyāb's daughter Manīzha, who falls in love with him. Afrāsiyāb,[108] referred to here by the poet as 'the prince of Turks', was the most prominent of the Turanian Turkish kings. When he discovers their illicit romance, Afrāsiyāb imprisons the hated Iranian hero Bīzhan in the well of Arzhang. Rustam, the renowned champion of the Iranian forces, eventually goes to Turan in disguise and rescues Bīzhan from the well, bringing Manīzha with him back to Iran.

Likewise, the Sufi poets consider the appearance of Jesus as an ever-reoccurring event sustaining them in the present, using in this context the metaphor of the 'Messiah's breath of inspiration' (*dam-i masīḥ*). Ḥāfiẓ alludes to this in two verses:

Love's physician is compassionate and endowed
With the breath of Jesus,
But whom should he assuage
If you are without pain?[109]

*

To whom may I relate such a subtlety?
She killed me—my stony-hearted mistress,
Yet possessed the life-giving breath of Jesus.[110]

Since God's grace is vouchsafed to the lover immediately in the present moment, the supplications and prayers offered up in the Religion of Love are neither to obtain welfare in the present here and now nor salvation in the future life. From the great archangels, whether they be Gabriel or Michael, down to the inhabitants of the fairy kingdom, denizens of the demon empire and the kingdom of the beasts, and then up to Satan's disobedience and pride, followed by Adam's sin and later repentance, along with all the graces and calamities sent by Heaven which have been recorded in holy scriptures about past communities—in the Religion of Love such circumstances fill the mystic's *presential awareness*. These legends are tangible issues of the present moment that facilitate the lover's pursuit of Eros, food for his soul that he consumes *hoc tempore* in the pursuit of knowledge, goodness and beauty, which incite him to excel in the only serious sport: *Amor*. Thus, for example, referring to Noah's Ark cast upon the flood, Ḥāfiẓ says:

> Don't desert your mates and quit the ark
> Of Noah, Ḥāfiẓ, else this typhoon of
> Vicissitudes shall blow your ship to bits.[111]

Conclusion

From the above review of the doctrine of the Religion of Love in classical Persian poetry, several conclusions may be drawn:

Firstly, it is clear that there is an actual religion—or faith—of love (*dīn yā madhhab-i ʿishq*) in Persian mystical literature. The proponents or prophets of this erotic faith comprise some of the greatest poets of the Persian language. They include the likes of Niẓāmī, Saʿdī, Rūmī, and Ḥāfiẓ, who have been sent by God-as-Eros charged with the mission of converting mankind to their philosophy of love.

In the second place, this religion of love is founded on principles of love innate within each human being, in accordance with the original disposition that God instilled within him that prompt him to pursue and love Beauty, Knowledge and Goodness.

Thirdly, this religion is not contrary to the tenets of any of the other divinely revealed religions of mankind. Anyone can become a votary of the religion of love regardless of previous socio-cultural conditioning, for conversion to love's creed lends new life to the faith which one already has.

Fourthly, this religion's essential message is one of friendship, affection, peace, and living with mutual toleration of others. The tranquillity and peace generated by love's faith also inculcates such basic values as courtesy, kindness, compassion and mutual respect of others.

Fifthly, the principles of this erotic faith appear in all the world's advanced cultures whether in East or West. Its prophets feature as the greatest poets, sages and saints of all the oriental and occidental civilizations.

Sixthly and lastly, the religion of love is the universal faith of all existing beings. From a cosmological standpoint, all beings, from the tiniest atom on up to the most complex of organisms, all things, whether animate or inanimate—all are followers of the religion of love, and ultimately whatever they do is subservient to Love's command. As Niẓāmī says:

Don't fall foul and get in trouble
 over these living, breathing idols.
They're demigods, yet worship not
 themselves, so follow not their cult.
Each wanders round caught up in a daze,
 distracted and dizzy as a compass;
They quest and probe throughout the east and west
 to seek the One from whom they're manifest.[112]

NOTES

1. *Man nakhvāham kard tark la'l-i yār u jām-i may/ Zāhidān ma'dhūr dārīdam ki īnam madhhab-ast. Dīwān-i Ḥāfiẓ*, ed. Parvīz Nātil Khānlarī (Tehran: Khwārazmī

1362 A.Hsh./1983), ghazal 30: 6. All renditions of the poetry in this essay unless otherwise indicated are by the translator.

2. Sa'īd Nafīsī, *Muḥīt-i zindigī va aḥwāl u ash'ār-i Rūdakī* (Tehran: Amīr Kabīr 1381 A.Hsh./2002), p. 503.

3. 'Ayn al-Quḍāt Hamadhānī, *Tamhīdāt*, edited by Afif Osseiran (Tehran: Manūchihrī 1341A.Hsh./ 1962), p. 22.

4. Ibid, *Tamhīdāt*, pp. 114-15.

5. *Dīvān-i Ḥakīm Abū'l-Majd Majdūd b. Ādam Sanā'ī Ghaznavī*, ed. Mudarris Raḍavī (Tehran: Intishārāt- Kitābkhāna Sanā'ī 1362 A.Hsh./1983), p. 913. *Az kīsh u ṭarīqatam chi pursī? 'Ishq-ast marā ṭarīqat u kīsh.*

6. Ibid, *Dīvān-I Sanā'ī*, p. 914.

7. Rūmī, *Kulliyāt-i Shams yā Dīvān-i Kabīr*, ed. B. Furūzānfar (Tehran: Amīr Kabīr 1976), IV, p. 225, ghazal 1992, v. 21067. I will revisit to Rūmī's teachings on love later on.

8. From his *Khusraw u Shīrīn*, in Waḥīd Dastgirdī (ed.), *Kulliyāt-i Ḥakīm Niẓāmī Ganjavī* (Tehran: Intishārāt- Bihzād 1378 A.Hsh./ 1999), p. 95 (12: 2-4).

9. *Khusraw u Shīrīn*, in ibid. p. 96 (12:23-25).

10. *Khusraw u Shīrīn*, in ibid. p. 96 (12:26-27).

11. See Koran II:33-34.

12. For further discussion of *dard* in 'Aṭṭār, see M.I. Waley, "Didactic Style and Self-Criticism in 'Aṭṭār," in in Leonard Lewisohn, Christopher Shackle (eds.), *'Attār and the Persian Sufi Tradition: the Art of Spiritual Flight* (London/New York: I.B Tauris, 2006, pp. 215-16. – Ed/Trans.

13. *Manṭiq al-ṭayr*, ed. Ṣādiq Gawharīn (Tehran: Intishārāt-i 'ilmī va farhangī 1342 A.Hsh/1963), p. 14, vv. 251-252. See also my introduction to my *Guzīda-yi Manṭiq al-ṭayr*, (Tehran: Intishārāt-i 'ilmī va farhangī 1373 A.Hsh/1994).

14. The translation featured here is by Michael Sells, *Stations of Desire: Love Elegies from Ibn 'Arabi* (Jerusalem: IBIS 2000), pp. 72-73; for the original Arabic, see Ibn 'Arabī, *The Tarjumán al-Ashwáq: A Collection of Mystical Odes*, ed. & trans. R.A. Nicholson (London: Theosophical Publishing House 1978), Ode XI, p. 19.

15. Translation by Th. Emil Homerin, *'Umar Ibn al-Fāriḍ: Sufi Verse, Saintly Life* (New York: Paulist Press 2001), pp. 47, 51.

16. Rūmī, *Kulliyāt-i Shams yā Dīvān-i Kabīr*, ed. B. Furūzānfar (Tehran: Amīr Kabīr 1976), V, p. 58, ghazal 2207, v. 23405. *Dar khulaṣa-yi 'ishq ākhar shīva-yi Islām kū? Dar kushūf-i mushkilātash ṣāḥib-i i'lām kū?*

17. Rūmī, *Kulliyāt-i Shams*, IV, pp. 150-51; 1869, vv. 19706-08, 197013-14. *Raw madhhab-i 'āshiq rā bar-'aks-i ravishhā dān, Kaz yār durūghīhā, az ṣidq bih u iḥsān. /*

Ḥāl-ast maḥāl-i ū, muzd-ast vabāl-i ū, 'Adl-ast hama-yi ẓulmash, dād-ast buhtān. / Narm-ast durūsht-i ū, Ka'ba-st kinisht-i ū, Khārī kay khalad dilbar, kwūshtar zih gul u rayḥān. / Gar ta'na zanī, gū'ī: 'Tu madhhab-i kazh dārī.' Man madhhab-i abrūyash bikhrīdam va dādam jān. / Z'īn madhhab-i kazh mastam, bas kardam u lab bastam, Bar dār-i dil-i rawshan, bāqiyash furū mīkhwān.

18. Rūmī, *Kulliyāt-i Shams*, VIII, p. 221, Quatrain 1314. *Mā madhhab-i chishm-i shūkh-i mastash dārīm. Kīsh-i sar-i zulf-i but-parastash dārīm. / Gūyand: 'Juz īn hard u buvad dīn-i durust.' Az 'dīn-i durust' mā shikastash dārīm.*

19. Rūmī, *Kulliyāt-i Shams*, VIII, p. 38, Quatrain 225. *Mā 'āshiq-i 'ishqīm u musalmān digar-ast. Mā mūr-i ḍa'īfīm un Sulaymān digar-ast. / Az mā rukh-i zard u jigar-pārih ṭalab. Bāzārchih-i qaṣab-furūshān digar-ast.*

20. Rūmī, *Kulliyāt-i Shams*, VIII, p. 130, Quatrain 767. *'Āshiq tu yaqīn dān kay Musalmān nabvad. Dar madhhab-i 'āshiq kufr u īmān nabvad. / Dar 'ishq, tan u 'aql u dil u jān nabvad. Har kas kay chinīn nagasht ū ān nabvad.*

21. *Mathnawi-yi ma'nawi*, ed. R.A. Nicholson (Rprt.: Tehran: Amir Kabir 1363 A.Hsh./ 1984), II: 1770.

22. *Dīwān-i Ḥāfiẓ*, ed. Khānlarī, ghazal 443: 1. Translation by Robert Bly and Leonard Lewisohn, *The Angels Knocking on the Tavern Door* (New York: HarperCollins 2008), p. 53.

23. *Dīwān-i Ḥāfiẓ*, ed. Khānlarī, ghazal 426: 5. Trans. Bly & Lewisohn, *Angels*, p. 49.

24. See also the essay by Leili Anvar 'The Radiance of Epiphany: the Vision of Beauty and Love in Ḥāfiẓ's Poem of Pre-Eternity', in L. Lewisohn (ed.), *Hafiz and the Religion of Love in Classical Persian Poetry* (London: I.B. Tauris, 2010), pp. 123-143– TRANS./ED.

25. *Dīwān-i Ḥāfiẓ*, ed. Khānlarī, ghazal 10: 8. *Rū-yi khūbat āyatī az luṭf bar mā kashf kard. Zān sabab juz luṭf u khūbī nīst dar tafsīr-i mā.*

26. *Dīwān-i Ḥāfiẓ*, ed. Khānlarī, ghazal 165: 4. *Mugh-bachchih-ī mīgudhasht, rahzan-i dīn u dil. Dar pay-i ān āshinā az hama bīgāna shud.*

27. As I have explained elsewhere: see my "Of Scent and Sweetness: 'Aṭṭār and his Legacy in Rūmī, Shabistarī and Ḥāfeẓ," in *'Aṭṭār and the Persian Sufi Tradition*, ed. Leonard Lewisohn and Christopher Shackle (London: I. B. Tauris, 2006), pp. 43-44.

28. *Dīwān-i Ḥāfiẓ*, ed. Khānlarī, ghazal 22: 1-4. Translation by Bly & Lewisohn, *Angels*, p. 78.

29. *Sharḥ-i 'irfānī ghazalhā-yi Ḥāfiẓ*, ed. Bahā' al-Dīn Khurramshāhī *et al.*, (Tehran: Nashr-i Qaṭra 1373 A.Hsh./ 1994), I, p. 428.

30. Ibid. Ṣamad Muwaḥḥid (ed.), *Majmū'a-i āthār-i Shaykh Maḥmūd Shabistarī*, (Tehran: Kitābkhāna-i Ṭahūrī 1365 A.Hsh./1986), p. 93, Gulshan-i rāz, vv. 626-28.

31. *Imshab may-i Jām yik manī khvāham kard. Khvud rā bi-raṭl-i may ghanī khvāham kard. / Awwal si ṭalāq 'aql u dīn khvāham kard. Pas dukhtar-i raz rā bi-zanī khvāham kard.*

32. *Rubáiyát of Omar Khayyam*, trans. Edward Fitzgerald, ed. R.A. Nicholson (London : Adam & Charles Black 1909), reprinted Tehran (Siphir 1384 A.Hsh./2005), with facing Persian texts, edited with an introduction by Huṣayn Ghomshei, Quatrain 40, p. 176.

33. *Dīwān-i Ḥāfiẓ*, ed. Khānlarī, ghazal 119: 7.

34. *Dīwān-i Ḥāfiẓ*, ed. Khānlarī, 193: 6.

35. *Dīwān-i Ḥāfiẓ*, ed. Khānlarī, 312: 1.

36. *Dīwān-i Ḥāfiẓ*, ed. Khānlarī, ghazal 213: 2; 426: 6 (*madhhab-i ṭarīqat*).

37. *Dīwān-i Ḥāfiẓ*, ed. Khānlarī, 133: 10.

38. *Dīwān-i Ḥāfiẓ*, ed. Khānlarī, ghazal 119: 7. Translation by Bly & Lewisohn, *Angels*, p. 48. *Sitam az ghamza miyāmūz ki dar madhhab-i 'ishq. Har 'amal ujrī va har karda jazā'ī dārad.*

39. *Dīwān-i Ḥāfiẓ*, ed. Khānlarī, ghazal 133: 10. *Bijuz abrū-yi tu miḥrāb-i dil-i Ḥāfiẓ nīst. Ṭā'at ghayr-i tu dar madhhab-i mā natavān kard.*

40. *Dīwān-i Ḥāfiẓ*, ed. Khānlarī, ghazal 48: 4. *Varā-yi ṭā'at-i dīvānagān zi mā maṭalab. Ki shaykh-i madhhab-i mā 'āqilī guna dānist.*

41. *Dīwān-i Ḥāfiẓ*, ed. Khānlarī, ghazal 193: 7. *Guftam sharāb u khirqa ni āyīn u madhhab-ast. Guft īn 'amal bi madhhab-i pīr-i mughān kunand.*

42. *Dīwān-i Ḥāfiẓ*, ed. Khānlarī, ghazal 312: 1. Translation by Bly & Lewisohn, *Angels*, p. 61. *Sālhā payravī madhhab-i rindān kardam, Tā bi-fatwā-yi khirad dīv bi-zindān kardam.*

43. *Dīwān-i Ḥāfiẓ*, ed. Khānlarī, ghazal 426: 6. *Dar madhhab-i ṭarīqat khāmī nishān-i kufr-ast. Ārī ṭarīq-i dawlat chālakī'st u chastī'st.*

44. Cited by William Chittick, *The Vision of Islam* (St. Paul, MN.: Paragon 1994), p. 138.

45. Other versions of this *ḥadīth* read: "Every child is born a Muslim..." See Neal Robinson, *The Sayings of Muhammad* (Hopewell, NJ: Ecco Press 1991), p. 13. The wider theological ramifications of this *ḥadīth* are explored in D.B. Macdonald, "Fiṭra," EI2, vol. 2, pp. 931f. – Tr.

46. *The Mathnawí of Jalálu'ddín Rúmí*, edited by R.A. Nicholson, (London: E.J.W. Gibb Memorial Trust 1924-40; rprt. Gibb Memorial Series N.S. 1971), I, 678-79. Translation by Alan Williams, *Rumi, Spiritual Verses: the First Book of the Masnavi-ye Ma'navi* (London: Penguin Books 2006), vv. 682-83, pp. 67-68.

47. *Mathnawī*, ed. Nicholson, IV: 409-14.

48. Shabistarī, *Gulshan-i rāz*, ed. Muwaḥḥid, vv. 418, 421, p. 84.

49. *Mathnawī*, VI:4541

50. *Kulliyāt-i Sa'dī*, ed. Muḥammad 'Alī Furūghī (Tehran: Amīr Kabīr 1363 A.Hsh./ 1984), ghazal 412 p. 761.

51. *Dīwān-i Ḥāfiẓ*, ed. Khānlarī, ghazal 137:4.

52. *Kulliyāt-i Sa'dī*, p. 203.

53. *Dīvān*, ed. Khānlarī, ghazal 174: 7. ('Wildman' has been used to render *qalandar* here)

54. On which, see M.G.S. Hodgson, 'Ibāḥa (II),' EI2, vol. 33, pp. 662-63. –Trans.

55. There are six instances where Ḥāfiẓ praises the *qalandar* and *qalandarī*: see *Dīwān-i Ḥāfiẓ*, ed. Khānlarī, ghazals 79: 7; 366:2; 389: 8; 479: 3; 174: 7; 442: 6. –Trans.

56. *Lā-ubālī chi kunad daftar-i dānā'ī rā. Ṭāqat-i va'ẓ nabāshad sar-i sawdā'ī rā./ 'Ashiqān rā chi gham az sar-zanash-i dushman u dūst? Yā gham-i dūst khurad ya gham-i rusvā'ī rā.* In *Kulliyāt-i Sa'dī*, p. 417.

57. *Gar murīd-i rāh-i 'ishqī fikr-i badnāmī makan. Shaykh Ṣan'ān khirqa rahn-i khāna-yi khammar dāsht.* In *Dīwān-i Ḥāfiẓ*, ghazal 79, v. 6.

58. *Dīwān-i Ḥāfiẓ*, ed. Khānlarī, ghazal 79: 6-7. *Waqt-i ān shīrīn-qalandar khvush ki dar aṭvār-i sayr, Dhikr-i tasbīḥ-i malak dar khalqa-i zunnār dāsht.*

59. *Dīwān-i Ḥāfiẓ*, ed. Khānlarī, ghazal 10: 8.

60. This idea is well-expressed in Blake's anecdote: 'Cowper came to me and said: 'O that I were insane always. I will never rest. Can you not make me truly insane? I will never rest till I am so. O that in the bosom of God I was hid.' *Blake: Complete Writings*, ed. G. Keynes (London: OUP 1972), p. 772. – Trans.

61. This is the purport of Shakespeare's verses in sonnet 53: 'Describe Adonis, and the counterfeit/ Is poorly imitated after you;/ On Helen's cheek all art of beauty set/ And you in Grecian tires are painted new; Speak of the spring, and the foison of the year:/ The one doth shadow of your beauty show,/ The other as your bounty doth appear,/ And you in every blessed shape we know.'

62. Rūmī, *Kulliyāt-i Shams*, ed. Furūzānfar, vol. 4, p. 302, ghazal 1620, v. 16957. *Havasī-ast dar sar-i man ki sar-i bashar nadāram. Man az īn havas chunānam ki zi khwud khabar nadāram.*

63. *Dīvān-i...Sanā'ī*, ed. Raḍavī, p. 546. *Bā nafasash siḥr-namāyān-i Hind. Dar havasash chihra-gushāyān-i Chīn.*

64. *Dīwān-i Ḥāfiẓ*, ed. Khānlarī, ghazal 261: 6. *'Ishq-bāzī kār-i bāzī nīst ay dil sar bibāz; var na gūyi 'ishq natvan zad bi-chūgān-i havas.*

65. *Dīwān-i Ḥāfiẓ*, ed. Khānlarī, ghazal 57: 8. *Ni īn zamān dil-i Ḥāfiẓ dar ātash-i havas ast, ki dāghdār-i azal hamchū lālih-i khvud-ru'ast.*

66. Rūmī, *Kulliyāt-i Shams*, ed. Furūzānfar, vol. 6, pp. 15-16 ghazal 2637, vv. 27975-78.

Imrūz samā'ast u sharāb-ast u ṣurāḥī; yik Sāqī-yi bad-mast, yikī jam'-i mubāḥī. / Zān jins-i mubāḥī kay az ān sū-yi wujūd-ast; nay ibāḥatī-yi gīj, hashīsh muzhājī. / [Rūḥī'st mubāḥī kay az ān rūḥ chishīda-ast. / Kū rūḥ-i qadīmī u kujā rūḥ-i riyāḥī. / Dar pīsh-i chinīn fitna va dar dast-i chinīn may: Yā Rabb! chih shavad jān-i musalmān-i ṣalāḥī.]

67. See the same ghazal 2637, v. 27986.

68. *Dīvān*, ed. Khānlarī, ghazal 278: 6. *Dilā dilālat-i khayrat kunam bi rāh-i najāt. Makan bi fisq mubāḥāt u zuhd ham mafarūsh.*

69. Rūmī, *Kulliyāt-i Shams*, ed. Furūzānfar, vol. 4, p. 36, ghazal 1685, v. 17660. *Dar jurm-i tawba kardan, būdīm tā bi gardan/ Az tawbahā-yi karda, īn bār tawba kardam.*

70. *Mathnawī-yi ma'nawī*, ed. R.A. Nicholson (Rprt.: Tehran: Amir Kabir 1984), VI: 897-902; 969-70.

71. *Mathnawī-yi ma'nawī*, VI: 969-70.

72. Rūmī, *Kulliyāt-i Shams*, ed. Furūzānfar, vol. 4, p. 66, ghazal 1735, v. 18199. *Zihī gunāh ki kufr-ast tawba kardan az ū/ Ni pas, ṭarīq-i gurīz va ni pīsh jā-yi maqām.*

73. *Kulliyāt-i Sa'dī*, p. 546

74. *Dīvān*, ed. Khānlarī, ghazal 20: 2. Translation by Robert Bly and Leonard Lewisohn, *The Angels Knocking on the Tavern Door: 30 Poems of Hafez* (New York: HarperCollins 2008), p. 59.

75. See my 'Of Scent and Sweetness'. In this volume pp. 83-117.

76. The original Persian reads *khūn-i jigar*, literally meaning 'the liver's blood,' but by extension signifies bitterly wept tears that are 'bloody tears torn from the heart,' or 'tears of blood drawn out of the gut.'

77. *Manṭiq al-ṭayr*, ed. Ṣādiq Gawharīn (Tehran: Intishārāt-i 'ilmī va farhangī 1342 A.Hsh/1963), vv. 1269-70; 1277-80; translation by Dick Davis and Afkham Darbandi, *The Conference of the Birds* (Middlesex, U.K.: Penguin 1984), pp. 61-62.

78. See 'Attar, *The Conference of the Birds*, trans. Afkham Darbandi and Dick Davis (Middlesex, U.K.: Penguin Books 1984), 'The Story of Shaykh San'an,' pp. 57-75.

79. On which, see: Javad Nurbakhsh, *Sufi Symbolism (The Nurbakhsh Encyclopedia of Sufi Terminology)*, vol. I, tr. L. Lewisohn & T. Graham (London, Khaniqahi Nimatullahi Publications 1986), See "Part 2: Sufi Symbolism of Wine, Music, Mystical Audition (*Samā'*) and Convivial Gatherings," pp. 125-214. – TRANS.

80. For a thorough discussion of this theme in Ḥāfiẓ's poetry, see Leili Anvar-Chenderoff's essay 'The Radiance of Epiphany: the Vision of Beauty and Love in Ḥāfiẓ's Poem of Pre-Eternity', in L. Lewisohn (ed.), *Hafiz and the Religion of Love in Classical Persian Poetry* (London: I.B. Tauris, 2010), pp. 123-143.

81. On the mystical theology of 'true idolatry' see L. Lewisohn, *Beyond Faith and*

Infidelity: the Sufi Poetry and Teachings of Mahmud Shabistari (Washingon, D.C.: IBEX 2009), chap. 8. – Trans.

82. *Mā dar piyāla 'aks-i rukh-i yār dīda-īm. Ay bīkhar zi ladhat-i shurb-i mudām-i mā*. In *Dīvān*, ed. Khānlarī, ghazal 11: 2.

83. *Kulliyāt-i Sa'dī*, ed. Furūghī, p. 545, ghazal 45:7

84. For further discussion of the role played by this key Qur'ānic motif in ⊠āfi⊠'s poems, see LeiliAnvar's essay in in L. Lewisohn (ed.), *Hafiz and the Religion of Love in Classical Persian Poetry* (London: I.B. Tauris, 2010), pp. 123-143. – Ed./Trans.

85. *Dīvān*, ed. Khānlarī, ghazal 273: 1 [reading *talkh* for *mast*] – Ed./Trans.

86. *Kulliyāt-i Sa'dī*, p. 509. This is similar to Alexander Pope's thesis at the conclusion of his *Essay on Man* (IV: 315-20) of the truth that 'Virtue alone is Happiness here below', describing Virtue as:

> The joy unequal'd, if its end it gain,
> And if it lose, attended with no pain:
> Without satiety, tho' ever so blest,
> And but more relish'd as the most distressed.
> The broadest mirth unfeeling Folly wears,
> Less pleasing far than Virtue's very tears. – Ed./Trans.

87. Translation by Robert Bly and Leonard Lewisohn, *Angels*, p. 48; *Dīvān*, ed. Khānlarī, ghazal 426: 9.

88. *Dīwān-i Ḥāfiẓ*, ed. Khānlarī, ghazal 21: 1

89. *Dīwān-i Ḥāfiẓ*, ed. Khānlarī, ghazal 22: 5

90. *Dīwān-i Ḥāfiẓ*, ed. Khānlarī, ghazal 144: 5.

91. From his *Sharaf-nāma*, in Waḥīd Dastgirdī (ed.), *Kulliyāt-i Ḥakīm Niẓāmī Ganjavī* (Tehran: Intishārāt-i Bihzād 1378 A.Hsh./ 1999), pp. 602 (7: 1-2); 615 (11: 1-2).

92. Trans. Homerin, *'Umar Ibn al-Fāriḍ: Sufi Verse*, p. 50.

93. *Mathnawī*, ed. Nicholson, I: 133.

94. *Mathnawī*, ed. Nicholson, III: 1433.

95. *Kitāb- Fihi mā fihi*, ed. Badī' al-Zamān Furūzānfar (Tehran : Amīr Kabīr 1348 A.Hsh./1969), p. 105; trans. A.J. Arberry, *The Discourses of Rumi* (Richmond : Curzon Press 1993 rprt.), p. 116.

96. *Dīwān-i Khwāja Ḥāfiẓ-i Shīrāzī*, ed. S. 'Abū'l-Qāsim Anjawī-Shīrāzī (Tehran: Sāzmān-i Intikhābāt-i Jāwidān 1358 A.Hsh./1979), p. 205. *Man ki imrūzam bihisht-i naqd ḥāṣil mishavad, Va'da-yi fardā-yi zāhid ra chirā bavar kunam?*

97. *Bakht-i javān dārad ānki bā tu qarīn ast/ Pīr nagardad ki dar bihisht-i barīn ast.* In *Kulliyāt-i Sa'dī*, p.571 ghazal 93:1.

98. *Mathnawī*, ed. Nicholson, IV: 3262

99. See Bahā al-Dīn Khurramshāhī (ed.), *Dānishnāma-yi Qur'ān*, (2nd printing; Tehran: Gulshan 1381/2002), s.v. 'Nimrūd', II, pp. 2273-74. - TRANS./ED.

100. See Jalāl al-Dīn Humā'ī, *Funūn-i balāghat va ṣanā'āt-i adabī* (24th ed., Tehran: Chāpkhāna-yi Ittiḥād 1382/2003), pp. 328-31; Browne, *Literary History of Persia*, II, pp. 77-80. - TRANS./ED.

101. *Dīwān-i Ḥāfiẓ*, ed. Khānlarī, ghazal 27: 2.

102. *Kulliyāt-i Sa'dī*, p. 551.

103. *Kulliyāt-i Sa'dī*, p. 568.

104. See H. Moayyad, 'Farhād,' *Encyclopedia Iranica*, IX, pp. 257–258. - TRANS/ED.

105. Chigil is a city near the Kazakhstan border not far from Kashgar in Xinjiang renowned for its beautiful women.

106. *Dīwān-i Ḥāfiẓ*, ed. Khānlarī, ghazal 461:5.

107. See Dj. Khaleghi-Motlagh, 'Bīžān,' *Encyclopedia Iranica*, IV, pp. 309–310. -TRANS./ED.

108. See E. Yarshater, ''Afrāsīāb,' *Encyclopedia Iranica*, I, pp. 570–576. -TRANS./ED

109. *Dīwān-i Ḥāfiẓ*, ed. Khānlarī, ghazal 182:4.

110. *Dīwān-i Ḥāfiẓ*, ed. Khānlarī, ghazal 59:6.

111. *Dīwān-i Ḥāfiẓ*, ed. Khānlarī, ghazal 19: 7. There is a reference to Koran, XXVI:119–20: 'And we saved him [Noah] and those with him in the laden ship. Then afterwards drowned the others.' —TRANS.

112. From his *Khusraw va Shīrīn*, in Waḥīd Dastgirdī (ed.), *Kulliyāt-i Ḥakīm Niẓāmī Ganjavī*, p. 81.